The Official Harvey Walsh

Trading Journal

Trade, Log, Analyze, Profit

The Official Harvey Walsh Trading Journal

Trade, Log, Analyze, Profit

First Published 2019 by Shelfless

First Edition [P1.0]

ISBN: 978-1697331004

Shelfless Ltd, Leigh-on-Sea, SS9 2AB, UK

WWW.SHELFLESS.CO.UK

Copyright © Harvey Walsh, 2019

The right of Harvey Walsh to be identified as author of this work has been asserted in accordance with sections 77 and 78 of the Copyright, Designs and Patents Act, 1988.

You may not copy, store, distribute, transmit, reproduce or otherwise make available this publication (or any part of it) in any form, or by any means (electronic, digital, optical, mechanical, photocopying, recording or otherwise), without the prior written permission of the publisher. Any person who does any unauthorised act in relation to this publication may be liable to criminal prosecution and civil claims for damages.

LIMIT OF LIABILITY / DISCLAIMER OF WARRANTY: THE PUBLISHER AND THE AUTHOR MAKE NO REPRESENTATIONS OR WARRANTIES WITH RESPECT TO THE ACCURACY OR COMPLETENESS OF THE CONTENTS OF THIS WORK AND SPECIFICALLY DISCLAIM ALL WARRANTIES, INCLUDING WITHOUT LIMITATION WARRANTIES OF FITNESS FOR A PARTICULAR PURPOSE. NO WARRANTY MAY BE CREATED OR EXTENDED BY SALES OR PROMOTIONAL MATERIALS. THE ADVICE AND STRATEGIES CONTAINED HEREIN MAY NOT BE SUITABLE FOR EVERY SITUATION. THIS WORK IS SOLD WITH THE UNDERSTANDING THAT THE PUBLISHER IS NOT ENGAGED IN RENDERING LEGAL, ACCOUNTING, FINANCIAL, INVESTMENT, OR OTHER PROFESSIONAL SERVICES. IF PROFESSIONAL ASSISTANCE IS REQUIRED, THE SERVICES OF A COMPETENT PROFESSIONAL PERSON SHOULD BE SOUGHT. NEITHER THE PUBLISHER NOR THE AUTHOR SHALL BE LIABLE FOR DAMAGES ARISING HERE FROM. THE FACT THAT AN ORGANISATION OR WEBSITE IS REFERRED TO IN THIS WORK AS A CITATION OR POTENTIAL SOURCE OF FURTHER INFORMATION DOES NOT MEAN THAT THE AUTHOR OR PUBLISHER ENDORSES THE INFORMATION THAT THE ORGANISATION OR WEBSITE MAY PROVIDE OR RECOMMENDATIONS IT MAY MAKE. FURTHERMORE, READERS SHOULD BE AWARE THAT INTERNET WEBSITES LISTED IN THIS WORK MAY HAVE CHANGED OR DISAPPEARED BETWEEN WHEN THIS WORK WAS WRITTEN AND WHEN IT IS READ.

Trading Books by Harvey Walsh

How To Day Trade Stocks For Profit is Harvey's highly acclaimed course designed to get you quickly making money from the stock market. No previous trading experience is necessary. Easy to read and jargon-free, it starts from the very basics, and builds to a remarkably simple but very powerful profit generating strategy.

Would you like to discover the forex trading strategies used by professional FX traders? In his second book, Harvey lifts the curtain and invites you into the lucrative world of currency trading. Written in his trademark plain English, this jargon-free course takes you through everything you need to know in order to start trading the foreign exchange market.

Your brain is your biggest barrier to success in the markets. It doesn't have to be this way. In this groundbreaking book, Harvey goes further than ever before in deconstructing the evolutionary developments and learned behaviours that have programmed us for failure in the markets. Discover his *brain hacks* – simple yet powerful tricks and techniques anyone can use to turn around their built-in disadvantages and use them to supercharge their trading.

The price of Bitcoin soared more than 1,300% in 2017. Not a bad return for anyone who bought at the start of the year, but savvy traders made considerably more. By trading price movements in both directions, those in the know were able to make huge profits, and in this book, Harvey shows you how you can do the same.

Contents

Introduction	1
Why Log?	3
The Importance of Firing Neurones	3
Execution is Everything	3
Analyse This	4
Further Benefits	4
Suggestions On Use	5
Planning	5
Trading	5
Goals & Rewards	7
Make It Yours	7
Trading Plan	8
Affirmations	10
Notes	11
Goals & Rewards	134

Introduction

As a day trader, trading coach, and author of four books on the subject, I've been privileged to work and communicate with traders all over the world. I've discussed strategy, talked technique, and examined tricks of the trade with the most successful of market participants. That knowledge has been distilled into my books, and has gone on to be used by thousands more traders around the globe. In all the books I have authored, there's one theme that comes up time and again — trade logging. Keeping a proper trading journal is not necessarily a prerequisite to success in the markets, but I don't know any profitable traders who *don't* keep one.

I'm a firm believer that trading is twenty percent about knowing what to do, and eighty percent about *actually doing it*. It sounds simple, but as anyone who trades knows, pulling the trigger on a trade, taking a loss without emotion, and waiting on the sidelines when the moment is not right, can be tough.

My books advocate the use of a journal because it's one of the best ways to achieve the *actually doing it* part of trading. Keeping a log not only enforces the discipline we need to keep us on track, it helps us to learn from our inevitable slip-ups and mistakes.

A good journal is so essential to trading successfully, I jumped at the chance when my publisher suggested I create a version of my own log book for others to use. The book you hold in your hands is the result of years of fine-tuning and tweaking. Until now I have only shared my personal log with a select few traders who have added their own suggestions and improvements. It is both time and battle tested, and has been my secret weapon for almost as long as I've been a profitable trader. It will, I hope, become an invaluable tool and a key part of your success as a trader too.

Why Log?

What's so special about writing down our trades? What good can possibly come from it? After all, the chances are our broker software lets us go back and see a list of our past entries and exits. So why take a few extra seconds to put pen to paper? And why even bother with pen and paper when we almost certainly have a keyboard in front of us when we are trading? Let's take that last question first.

The Importance of Firing Neurones

The act of writing — of physically pushing a pen or a pencil around a piece of paper — is *cognitively expensive*. That's a fancy way of saying that it uses more brainpower than hammering a few keys on a keyboard. This is important for two reasons:

1) The more neurones involved in a task, the more our chance of remembering the task. Memories are built from connections between neurones. Use more, and the memory is stronger. So by writing something down longhand, there is a greater chance we will remember it.

2) Using more of our neurones on one task means there are fewer available for other things. So by concentrating our available brainpower on writing something down, we are forcing ourselves to think clearly and with focus about what it is we are writing.

What this means in practice is that when we write down a trade on paper, we will think with clarity and focus about what we are writing, which in turn means we will take a moment to consider the trade properly. In short, writing down trades makes us think about them rather than mindlessly bashing buy and sell buttons.

Execution is Everything

If you've read any of my other books, you'll know I am a big believer in focussing on trade execution above all else. We cannot control the markets, we can't make a price move the way we want it to. There's no point trying to influence something outside our control and there's no point in getting upset if a trade turns into a loss. Equally, we shouldn't necessarily be giving ourselves a pat on the back every time we bag a winner.

The one and only thing we *can* control is our execution, and it's important to remind ourselves of that and to improve it constantly. Only by striving to execute every trade perfectly can we hope to profit when market conditions allow, and to minimise our losses when they don't.

That's why this journal encourages the scoring or grading of each trade setup, and each trade execution. Recording these scores means we can go back and analyse our performance rather than study the misleading metric of our profit or loss. It's entirely possible for us to do everything right and still lose money. It's also quite possible to do everything wrong and still make a bit of money by luck. Unless we record what really matters — our execution — we could be beating ourselves up needlessly, or heaping unwarranted congratulations on ourselves.

Analyse This

The benefits of journaling begin the moment we put pen to paper, an act which as we've seen, forces us to truly consider the trade at hand. An even bigger benefit comes from going back through the journal and analysing it. In the heat of the moment, when we have live charts in front of us and money on the line, it's easy to persuade ourselves we are doing the right thing, that the trade is a good one and we really should be holding our position.

If we go back to our trade log later, ideally after at least one night's sleep so we are emotionally detached from the action, we can see the true state of our work laid bare. That trade that looked so good when our finger was hovering over the buy button? What were we thinking! In the cold light of day, devoid of adrenaline and the need to turn a profit, we can see it for the lemon it was. Our trade log will give us an insight into what we were thinking at the time. By analysing our thought process, and our execution, we can see where we are going wrong and take steps to put things right. If we perfect our execution, profit becomes inevitable.

Further Benefits

There are more benefits to trade logging, and using the other sections of this journal, than I can reasonably go into here. There is a deep discussion in my book *Brain Hacks For Traders*. If you are interested in hacking the cognitive biases and learned behaviours that could be negatively impacting your ability to execute, I humbly recommend giving it a read. Briefly though, some other benefits of using this journal include:

- Hacking illusory correlation
- Building a shield against apophenia and other 'monsters' lurking behind the screen
- Avoiding hyperbolic discounting
- Conquering over-trading
- Managing chunking and blocking
- Hacking the reward system

Suggestions On Use

How you use this trading journal is, of course, entirely up to you. However, as it is based around my own research, experience, and the content of my other books, it would be remiss of me not to make some suggestions on usage and to explain the thinking behind the various sections.

The journal is split into three parts: *planning*, *trading*, and *goals and rewards*.

Planning

These free-form pages are a place for you to set out your trading plan, with space for written rules and drawn setups. A good plan usually includes a description of what you are trading and how you should be trading it. I keep a list of setups and model trades in my plan, and I go through it at the start of each week to remind myself to trade only setups that are tried and tested and that I know work. If you have any rules you want to follow, this is the place to write them down.

There is also space here to write down positive affirmations. Neuro Linguistic Programming, or NLP, is a powerful brain hack, and reading through a couple of affirmations before each trading session is a useful exercise.

Trading

The trading section is set out as a series of double-page spreads. As this journal is designed with day trading in mind, it has been laid out so that each new day starts on a new pair of pages. If you are trading over a different time-frame, you can use the pages in any way that works for you.

The left-hand page of each spread is where you can fill in any pre-market and post-market information you wish to record. I've provided the following sections:

Date, and *Paper / Live* checkboxes. Tick accordingly to remind yourself when you come back and analyse your log, whether or not real money was on the line.

Watchlist. A place to list the symbols you will be watching. This is of particular interest to stock traders.

Market Events. If there are any upcoming economic announcements or other events that could impact the trading day, they can be noted here so you have them at hand while working.

Goals & Rewards. A place to define any daily goals and associated rewards. This can be used in conjunction with...

Reward circles. Gamification of trading is one of the most powerful brain hacks I know. Disconnecting trading from profit and instead creating a link between excellent execution and some form of reward, is the best way to train our brain to focus on and improve execution. Shade one of these circles, or put a cross in one, whenever you give yourself a perfect score (5) for executing a trade. If you get enough circles, give yourself the reward you recorded in the Goals & Rewards box. Writing down the reward *before* you start trading means you can't cheat later.

Pre-Market Observations. A free space to jot down anything you think may impact the trading session ahead. That could be market conditions, environmental conditions, your own state of mind, anything that could have an effect on your trading.

Post-Market Observations. This is a space to note anything you want to remember once trading is over and the session is still fresh in your mind.

Checkboxes for post-trading review. This journal will be infinitely more useful if you spend time away from the market to go through and analyse it. I recommend reading through the previous session's trades before starting a new session, and also reading through a second time at the end of the week.

The right-hand page of each spread is for logging individual trades. Obviously you do not have to fill in all the sections, but I've provided space to record the following:

The *symbol* being traded.

The *setup* being traded. I recommend having abbreviations for each setup in your trading plan so that you can note them quickly.

A *setup score* out of 5. Clearly not every setup is going to be perfect, so grading them before entry will allow you to go back later and determine just how marginal a setup can be for it to be considered worthy of entering.

Direction checkboxes for *Long or Short*.

Entry and *exit*. These boxes have been left large enough to let you record price, time, and slippage in as much or as little detail as you want. The *exit* box is larger to allow for scaling out of trades.

Position size.

The reason for exiting. There are checkboxes to tick quickly if the reason for exiting was the trade reaching its target (*TGT*) or a stop loss (*SL*) being hit.

Execution score. Probably the most important space on the page. Give yourself a 5 and a pat on the back if you did everything correctly, regardless of whether the trade was profitable. Knock off a point for anything that left room for improvement. If you saw a setup but failed to trade it, score 0.

Notes. A free-form section to record anything else pertinent to your own trading strategy.

Goals & Rewards

As I mentioned above, disconnecting execution from profit and using an independent system of rewards to encourage excellence in the one thing we can control — execution — is one of the most effective techniques I know for becoming a better trader. When execution is perfect, provided we are trading a proven strategy with positive expectancy, profit becomes inevitable.

Writing down your goals and rewards before you take a single trade means you can't cheat and decide to reward yourself randomly just because you feel you had a good day.

I've added an extra couple of pages at the back of the journal where you can set yourself various longer-term goals and associate rewards with them. For example, you might decide that if ninety percent of your trades for a week get a 5/5 execution score, you will take a trip to the movies, or have a meal out.

Make It Yours

I want to re-iterate that these suggestions are based on how I log my trades as a day trader. They are just that — suggestions. Maybe they'll work for you, or maybe you don't want to keep such detailed records. Maybe gamification isn't for you, or perhaps you trade a single futures contract and don't need space for a watchlist. Whatever kind of trader you are, make this journal your own and use it in a way that makes sense for you. There's no right or wrong way to use this book, there's just *your* way.

I wish you good trading!

Trading Plan

Trading Plan

Affirmations

Notes

Date	☐ Paper ☐ Live	Watchlist

Market Events

Goals & Rewards

Pre-Market Observations

○ ○ ○ ○ ○ ○ ○ ○ ○ ○ ○

Post-Market Observations

☐ 24 Hour Review   ☐ End of Week Review   ☐ End of Month Review

Symbol	Setup Score	☐ L	Entry	Position Size	☐ TGT ☐ S/L	Execution Score
Setup		☐ S	Exit			

Symbol	Setup Score	☐ L	Entry	Position Size	☐ TGT ☐ S/L	Execution Score
Setup		☐ S	Exit			

Symbol	Setup Score	☐ L	Entry	Position Size	☐ TGT ☐ S/L	Execution Score
Setup		☐ S	Exit			

Symbol	Setup Score	☐ L	Entry	Position Size	☐ TGT ☐ S/L	Execution Score
Setup		☐ S	Exit			

Symbol	Setup Score	☐ L	Entry	Position Size	☐ TGT ☐ S/L	Execution Score
Setup		☐ S	Exit			

Symbol	Setup Score	☐ L	Entry	Position Size	☐ TGT ☐ S/L	Execution Score
Setup		☐ S	Exit			

Symbol	Setup Score	☐ L	Entry	Position Size	☐ TGT ☐ S/L	Execution Score
Setup		☐ S	Exit			

Symbol	Setup Score	☐ L	Entry	Position Size	☐ TGT ☐ S/L	Execution Score
Setup		☐ S	Exit			

Symbol	Setup Score	☐ L	Entry	Position Size	☐ TGT ☐ S/L	Execution Score
Setup		☐ S	Exit			

Symbol	Setup Score	☐ L	Entry	Position Size	☐ TGT ☐ S/L	Execution Score
Setup		☐ S	Exit			

| Date | ☐ Paper ☐ Live | Watchlist |

Market Events

Goals & Rewards

Pre-Market Observations

◯ ◯ ◯ ◯ ◯ ◯ ◯ ◯ ◯ ◯ ◯

Post-Market Observations

☐ 24 Hour Review   ☐ End of Week Review   ☐ End of Month Review

Symbol	Setup Score	☐ L	Entry	Position Size	☐ TGT ☐ S/L	Execution Score
Setup		☐ S	Exit			

Symbol	Setup Score	☐ L	Entry	Position Size	☐ TGT ☐ S/L	Execution Score
Setup		☐ S	Exit			

Symbol	Setup Score	☐ L	Entry	Position Size	☐ TGT ☐ S/L	Execution Score
Setup		☐ S	Exit			

Symbol	Setup Score	☐ L	Entry	Position Size	☐ TGT ☐ S/L	Execution Score
Setup		☐ S	Exit			

Symbol	Setup Score	☐ L	Entry	Position Size	☐ TGT ☐ S/L	Execution Score
Setup		☐ S	Exit			

Symbol	Setup Score	☐ L	Entry	Position Size	☐ TGT ☐ S/L	Execution Score
Setup		☐ S	Exit			

Symbol	Setup Score	☐ L	Entry	Position Size	☐ TGT ☐ S/L	Execution Score
Setup		☐ S	Exit			

Symbol	Setup Score	☐ L	Entry	Position Size	☐ TGT ☐ S/L	Execution Score
Setup		☐ S	Exit			

Symbol	Setup Score	☐ L	Entry	Position Size	☐ TGT ☐ S/L	Execution Score
Setup		☐ S	Exit			

Symbol	Setup Score	☐ L	Entry	Position Size	☐ TGT ☐ S/L	Execution Score
Setup		☐ S	Exit			

| Date | ☐ Paper ☐ Live | Watchlist |

Market Events

Goals & Rewards

Pre-Market Observations

○ ○ ○ ○ ○ ○ ○ ○ ○ ○

Post-Market Observations

☐ 24 Hour Review ☐ End of Week Review ☐ End of Month Review

Symbol	Setup Score	☐ L	Entry	Position Size	☐ TGT ☐ S/L	Execution Score
Setup		☐ S	Exit			

Symbol	Setup Score	☐ L	Entry	Position Size	☐ TGT ☐ S/L	Execution Score
Setup		☐ S	Exit			

Symbol	Setup Score	☐ L	Entry	Position Size	☐ TGT ☐ S/L	Execution Score
Setup		☐ S	Exit			

Symbol	Setup Score	☐ L	Entry	Position Size	☐ TGT ☐ S/L	Execution Score
Setup		☐ S	Exit			

Symbol	Setup Score	☐ L	Entry	Position Size	☐ TGT ☐ S/L	Execution Score
Setup		☐ S	Exit			

Symbol	Setup Score	☐ L	Entry	Position Size	☐ TGT ☐ S/L	Execution Score
Setup		☐ S	Exit			

Symbol	Setup Score	☐ L	Entry	Position Size	☐ TGT ☐ S/L	Execution Score
Setup		☐ S	Exit			

Symbol	Setup Score	☐ L	Entry	Position Size	☐ TGT ☐ S/L	Execution Score
Setup		☐ S	Exit			

Symbol	Setup Score	☐ L	Entry	Position Size	☐ TGT ☐ S/L	Execution Score
Setup		☐ S	Exit			

Symbol	Setup Score	☐ L	Entry	Position Size	☐ TGT ☐ S/L	Execution Score
Setup		☐ S	Exit			

Date ☐ Paper ☐ Live

Watchlist

Market Events

Goals & Rewards

Pre-Market Observations

Post-Market Observations

☐ 24 Hour Review   ☐ End of Week Review   ☐ End of Month Review

Symbol	Setup Score	☐ L	Entry	Position Size	☐ TGT ☐ S/L	Execution Score
Setup		☐ S	Exit			

Symbol	Setup Score	☐ L	Entry	Position Size	☐ TGT ☐ S/L	Execution Score
Setup		☐ S	Exit			

Symbol	Setup Score	☐ L	Entry	Position Size	☐ TGT ☐ S/L	Execution Score
Setup		☐ S	Exit			

Symbol	Setup Score	☐ L	Entry	Position Size	☐ TGT ☐ S/L	Execution Score
Setup		☐ S	Exit			

Symbol	Setup Score	☐ L	Entry	Position Size	☐ TGT ☐ S/L	Execution Score
Setup		☐ S	Exit			

Symbol	Setup Score	☐ L	Entry	Position Size	☐ TGT ☐ S/L	Execution Score
Setup		☐ S	Exit			

Symbol	Setup Score	☐ L	Entry	Position Size	☐ TGT ☐ S/L	Execution Score
Setup		☐ S	Exit			

Symbol	Setup Score	☐ L	Entry	Position Size	☐ TGT ☐ S/L	Execution Score
Setup		☐ S	Exit			

Symbol	Setup Score	☐ L	Entry	Position Size	☐ TGT ☐ S/L	Execution Score
Setup		☐ S	Exit			

Symbol	Setup Score	☐ L	Entry	Position Size	☐ TGT ☐ S/L	Execution Score
Setup		☐ S	Exit			

Date   ☐ Paper   ☐ Live

Watchlist

Market Events

Goals & Rewards

Pre-Market Observations

○ ○ ○ ○ ○ ○ ○ ○ ○ ○ ○

Post-Market Observations

☐ 24 Hour Review   ☐ End of Week Review   ☐ End of Month Review

Symbol	Setup Score	☐ L	Entry	Position Size	☐ TGT ☐ S/L	Execution Score
Setup		☐ S	Exit			

Symbol	Setup Score	☐ L	Entry	Position Size	☐ TGT ☐ S/L	Execution Score
Setup		☐ S	Exit			

Symbol	Setup Score	☐ L	Entry	Position Size	☐ TGT ☐ S/L	Execution Score
Setup		☐ S	Exit			

Symbol	Setup Score	☐ L	Entry	Position Size	☐ TGT ☐ S/L	Execution Score
Setup		☐ S	Exit			

Symbol	Setup Score	☐ L	Entry	Position Size	☐ TGT ☐ S/L	Execution Score
Setup		☐ S	Exit			

Symbol	Setup Score	☐ L	Entry	Position Size	☐ TGT ☐ S/L	Execution Score
Setup		☐ S	Exit			

Symbol	Setup Score	☐ L	Entry	Position Size	☐ TGT ☐ S/L	Execution Score
Setup		☐ S	Exit			

Symbol	Setup Score	☐ L	Entry	Position Size	☐ TGT ☐ S/L	Execution Score
Setup		☐ S	Exit			

Symbol	Setup Score	☐ L	Entry	Position Size	☐ TGT ☐ S/L	Execution Score
Setup		☐ S	Exit			

Symbol	Setup Score	☐ L	Entry	Position Size	☐ TGT ☐ S/L	Execution Score
Setup		☐ S	Exit			

| Date | ☐ Paper ☐ Live | Watchlist |

Market Events

Goals & Rewards

Pre-Market Observations

○ ○ ○ ○ ○ ○ ○ ○ ○ ○

Post-Market Observations

☐ 24 Hour Review   ☐ End of Week Review   ☐ End of Month Review

Symbol	Setup Score	☐ L	Entry	Position Size	☐ TGT ☐ S/L	Execution Score
Setup		☐ S	Exit			

Symbol	Setup Score	☐ L	Entry	Position Size	☐ TGT ☐ S/L	Execution Score
Setup		☐ S	Exit			

Symbol	Setup Score	☐ L	Entry	Position Size	☐ TGT ☐ S/L	Execution Score
Setup		☐ S	Exit			

Symbol	Setup Score	☐ L	Entry	Position Size	☐ TGT ☐ S/L	Execution Score
Setup		☐ S	Exit			

Symbol	Setup Score	☐ L	Entry	Position Size	☐ TGT ☐ S/L	Execution Score
Setup		☐ S	Exit			

Symbol	Setup Score	☐ L	Entry	Position Size	☐ TGT ☐ S/L	Execution Score
Setup		☐ S	Exit			

Symbol	Setup Score	☐ L	Entry	Position Size	☐ TGT ☐ S/L	Execution Score
Setup		☐ S	Exit			

Symbol	Setup Score	☐ L	Entry	Position Size	☐ TGT ☐ S/L	Execution Score
Setup		☐ S	Exit			

Symbol	Setup Score	☐ L	Entry	Position Size	☐ TGT ☐ S/L	Execution Score
Setup		☐ S	Exit			

Symbol	Setup Score	☐ L	Entry	Position Size	☐ TGT ☐ S/L	Execution Score
Setup		☐ S	Exit			

| Date | ☐ Paper ☐ Live | Watchlist |

Market Events

Goals & Rewards

Pre-Market Observations

○ ○ ○ ○ ○ ○ ○ ○ ○ ○

Post-Market Observations

☐ 24 Hour Review   ☐ End of Week Review   ☐ End of Month Review

Symbol	Setup Score	☐ L	Entry	Position Size	☐ TGT ☐ S/L	Execution Score
Setup		☐ S	Exit			

Symbol	Setup Score	☐ L	Entry	Position Size	☐ TGT ☐ S/L	Execution Score
Setup		☐ S	Exit			

Symbol	Setup Score	☐ L	Entry	Position Size	☐ TGT ☐ S/L	Execution Score
Setup		☐ S	Exit			

Symbol	Setup Score	☐ L	Entry	Position Size	☐ TGT ☐ S/L	Execution Score
Setup		☐ S	Exit			

Symbol	Setup Score	☐ L	Entry	Position Size	☐ TGT ☐ S/L	Execution Score
Setup		☐ S	Exit			

Symbol	Setup Score	☐ L	Entry	Position Size	☐ TGT ☐ S/L	Execution Score
Setup		☐ S	Exit			

Symbol	Setup Score	☐ L	Entry	Position Size	☐ TGT ☐ S/L	Execution Score
Setup		☐ S	Exit			

Symbol	Setup Score	☐ L	Entry	Position Size	☐ TGT ☐ S/L	Execution Score
Setup		☐ S	Exit			

Symbol	Setup Score	☐ L	Entry	Position Size	☐ TGT ☐ S/L	Execution Score
Setup		☐ S	Exit			

Symbol	Setup Score	☐ L	Entry	Position Size	☐ TGT ☐ S/L	Execution Score
Setup		☐ S	Exit			

Date	☐ Paper ☐ Live	Watchlist

Market Events

Goals & Rewards

Pre-Market Observations

○ ○ ○ ○ ○ ○ ○ ○ ○ ○

Post-Market Observations

☐ 24 Hour Review   ☐ End of Week Review   ☐ End of Month Review

Symbol	Setup Score	☐ L	Entry	Position Size	☐ TGT ☐ S/L	Execution Score
Setup		☐ S	Exit			

Symbol	Setup Score	☐ L	Entry	Position Size	☐ TGT ☐ S/L	Execution Score
Setup		☐ S	Exit			

Symbol	Setup Score	☐ L	Entry	Position Size	☐ TGT ☐ S/L	Execution Score
Setup		☐ S	Exit			

Symbol	Setup Score	☐ L	Entry	Position Size	☐ TGT ☐ S/L	Execution Score
Setup		☐ S	Exit			

Symbol	Setup Score	☐ L	Entry	Position Size	☐ TGT ☐ S/L	Execution Score
Setup		☐ S	Exit			

Symbol	Setup Score	☐ L	Entry	Position Size	☐ TGT ☐ S/L	Execution Score
Setup		☐ S	Exit			

Symbol	Setup Score	☐ L	Entry	Position Size	☐ TGT ☐ S/L	Execution Score
Setup		☐ S	Exit			

Symbol	Setup Score	☐ L	Entry	Position Size	☐ TGT ☐ S/L	Execution Score
Setup		☐ S	Exit			

Symbol	Setup Score	☐ L	Entry	Position Size	☐ TGT ☐ S/L	Execution Score
Setup		☐ S	Exit			

Symbol	Setup Score	☐ L	Entry	Position Size	☐ TGT ☐ S/L	Execution Score
Setup		☐ S	Exit			

| Date | ☐ Paper ☐ Live | Watchlist |

Market Events

Goals & Rewards

Pre-Market Observations

○ ○ ○ ○ ○ ○ ○ ○ ○ ○ ○

Post-Market Observations

☐ 24 Hour Review ☐ End of Week Review ☐ End of Month Review

Symbol	Setup Score	☐ L	Entry	Position Size	☐ TGT ☐ S/L	Execution Score
Setup		☐ S	Exit			

Symbol	Setup Score	☐ L	Entry	Position Size	☐ TGT ☐ S/L	Execution Score
Setup		☐ S	Exit			

Symbol	Setup Score	☐ L	Entry	Position Size	☐ TGT ☐ S/L	Execution Score
Setup		☐ S	Exit			

Symbol	Setup Score	☐ L	Entry	Position Size	☐ TGT ☐ S/L	Execution Score
Setup		☐ S	Exit			

Symbol	Setup Score	☐ L	Entry	Position Size	☐ TGT ☐ S/L	Execution Score
Setup		☐ S	Exit			

Symbol	Setup Score	☐ L	Entry	Position Size	☐ TGT ☐ S/L	Execution Score
Setup		☐ S	Exit			

Symbol	Setup Score	☐ L	Entry	Position Size	☐ TGT ☐ S/L	Execution Score
Setup		☐ S	Exit			

Symbol	Setup Score	☐ L	Entry	Position Size	☐ TGT ☐ S/L	Execution Score
Setup		☐ S	Exit			

Symbol	Setup Score	☐ L	Entry	Position Size	☐ TGT ☐ S/L	Execution Score
Setup		☐ S	Exit			

Symbol	Setup Score	☐ L	Entry	Position Size	☐ TGT ☐ S/L	Execution Score
Setup		☐ S	Exit			

| Date | ☐ Paper ☐ Live | Watchlist |

Market Events

Goals & Rewards

Pre-Market Observations

○ ○ ○ ○ ○ ○ ○ ○ ○ ○ ○

Post-Market Observations

☐ 24 Hour Review   ☐ End of Week Review   ☐ End of Month Review

Symbol	Setup Score	☐ L	Entry	Position Size	☐ TGT ☐ S/L	Execution Score
Setup		☐ S	Exit			

Symbol	Setup Score	☐ L	Entry	Position Size	☐ TGT ☐ S/L	Execution Score
Setup		☐ S	Exit			

Symbol	Setup Score	☐ L	Entry	Position Size	☐ TGT ☐ S/L	Execution Score
Setup		☐ S	Exit			

Symbol	Setup Score	☐ L	Entry	Position Size	☐ TGT ☐ S/L	Execution Score
Setup		☐ S	Exit			

Symbol	Setup Score	☐ L	Entry	Position Size	☐ TGT ☐ S/L	Execution Score
Setup		☐ S	Exit			

Symbol	Setup Score	☐ L	Entry	Position Size	☐ TGT ☐ S/L	Execution Score
Setup		☐ S	Exit			

Symbol	Setup Score	☐ L	Entry	Position Size	☐ TGT ☐ S/L	Execution Score
Setup		☐ S	Exit			

Symbol	Setup Score	☐ L	Entry	Position Size	☐ TGT ☐ S/L	Execution Score
Setup		☐ S	Exit			

Symbol	Setup Score	☐ L	Entry	Position Size	☐ TGT ☐ S/L	Execution Score
Setup		☐ S	Exit			

Symbol	Setup Score	☐ L	Entry	Position Size	☐ TGT ☐ S/L	Execution Score
Setup		☐ S	Exit			

Date	☐ Paper ☐ Live	Watchlist

Market Events

Goals & Rewards

Pre-Market Observations

◯ ◯ ◯ ◯ ◯ ◯ ◯ ◯ ◯ ◯

Post-Market Observations

☐ 24 Hour Review   ☐ End of Week Review   ☐ End of Month Review

Symbol	Setup Score	☐ L	Entry	Position Size	☐ TGT ☐ S/L	Execution Score
Setup		☐ S	Exit			

Symbol	Setup Score	☐ L	Entry	Position Size	☐ TGT ☐ S/L	Execution Score
Setup		☐ S	Exit			

Symbol	Setup Score	☐ L	Entry	Position Size	☐ TGT ☐ S/L	Execution Score
Setup		☐ S	Exit			

Symbol	Setup Score	☐ L	Entry	Position Size	☐ TGT ☐ S/L	Execution Score
Setup		☐ S	Exit			

Symbol	Setup Score	☐ L	Entry	Position Size	☐ TGT ☐ S/L	Execution Score
Setup		☐ S	Exit			

Symbol	Setup Score	☐ L	Entry	Position Size	☐ TGT ☐ S/L	Execution Score
Setup		☐ S	Exit			

Symbol	Setup Score	☐ L	Entry	Position Size	☐ TGT ☐ S/L	Execution Score
Setup		☐ S	Exit			

Symbol	Setup Score	☐ L	Entry	Position Size	☐ TGT ☐ S/L	Execution Score
Setup		☐ S	Exit			

Symbol	Setup Score	☐ L	Entry	Position Size	☐ TGT ☐ S/L	Execution Score
Setup		☐ S	Exit			

Symbol	Setup Score	☐ L	Entry	Position Size	☐ TGT ☐ S/L	Execution Score
Setup		☐ S	Exit			

Date ☐ Paper ☐ Live

Watchlist

Market Events

Goals & Rewards

Pre-Market Observations

Post-Market Observations

☐ 24 Hour Review   ☐ End of Week Review   ☐ End of Month Review

Symbol	Setup Score	☐ L	Entry	Position Size	☐ TGT ☐ S/L	Execution Score
Setup		☐ S	Exit			

Symbol	Setup Score	☐ L	Entry	Position Size	☐ TGT ☐ S/L	Execution Score
Setup		☐ S	Exit			

Symbol	Setup Score	☐ L	Entry	Position Size	☐ TGT ☐ S/L	Execution Score
Setup		☐ S	Exit			

Symbol	Setup Score	☐ L	Entry	Position Size	☐ TGT ☐ S/L	Execution Score
Setup		☐ S	Exit			

Symbol	Setup Score	☐ L	Entry	Position Size	☐ TGT ☐ S/L	Execution Score
Setup		☐ S	Exit			

Symbol	Setup Score	☐ L	Entry	Position Size	☐ TGT ☐ S/L	Execution Score
Setup		☐ S	Exit			

Symbol	Setup Score	☐ L	Entry	Position Size	☐ TGT ☐ S/L	Execution Score
Setup		☐ S	Exit			

Symbol	Setup Score	☐ L	Entry	Position Size	☐ TGT ☐ S/L	Execution Score
Setup		☐ S	Exit			

Symbol	Setup Score	☐ L	Entry	Position Size	☐ TGT ☐ S/L	Execution Score
Setup		☐ S	Exit			

Symbol	Setup Score	☐ L	Entry	Position Size	☐ TGT ☐ S/L	Execution Score
Setup		☐ S	Exit			

Date　　☐ Paper　☐ Live

Watchlist

Market Events

Goals & Rewards

Pre-Market Observations

◯ ◯ ◯ ◯ ◯ ◯ ◯ ◯ ◯ ◯

Post-Market Observations

☐ 24 Hour Review　☐ End of Week Review　☐ End of Month Review

Symbol	Setup Score	☐ L	Entry	Position Size	☐ TGT ☐ S/L	Execution Score
Setup		☐ S	Exit			

Symbol	Setup Score	☐ L	Entry	Position Size	☐ TGT ☐ S/L	Execution Score
Setup		☐ S	Exit			

Symbol	Setup Score	☐ L	Entry	Position Size	☐ TGT ☐ S/L	Execution Score
Setup		☐ S	Exit			

Symbol	Setup Score	☐ L	Entry	Position Size	☐ TGT ☐ S/L	Execution Score
Setup		☐ S	Exit			

Symbol	Setup Score	☐ L	Entry	Position Size	☐ TGT ☐ S/L	Execution Score
Setup		☐ S	Exit			

Symbol	Setup Score	☐ L	Entry	Position Size	☐ TGT ☐ S/L	Execution Score
Setup		☐ S	Exit			

Symbol	Setup Score	☐ L	Entry	Position Size	☐ TGT ☐ S/L	Execution Score
Setup		☐ S	Exit			

Symbol	Setup Score	☐ L	Entry	Position Size	☐ TGT ☐ S/L	Execution Score
Setup		☐ S	Exit			

Symbol	Setup Score	☐ L	Entry	Position Size	☐ TGT ☐ S/L	Execution Score
Setup		☐ S	Exit			

Symbol	Setup Score	☐ L	Entry	Position Size	☐ TGT ☐ S/L	Execution Score
Setup		☐ S	Exit			

Date | ☐ Paper ☐ Live

Watchlist

Market Events

Goals & Rewards

Pre-Market Observations

○ ○ ○ ○ ○ ○ ○ ○ ○ ○

Post-Market Observations

☐ 24 Hour Review   ☐ End of Week Review   ☐ End of Month Review

Symbol	Setup Score	☐ L	Entry	Position Size	☐ TGT ☐ S/L	Execution Score
Setup		☐ S	Exit			

Symbol	Setup Score	☐ L	Entry	Position Size	☐ TGT ☐ S/L	Execution Score
Setup		☐ S	Exit			

Symbol	Setup Score	☐ L	Entry	Position Size	☐ TGT ☐ S/L	Execution Score
Setup		☐ S	Exit			

Symbol	Setup Score	☐ L	Entry	Position Size	☐ TGT ☐ S/L	Execution Score
Setup		☐ S	Exit			

Symbol	Setup Score	☐ L	Entry	Position Size	☐ TGT ☐ S/L	Execution Score
Setup		☐ S	Exit			

Symbol	Setup Score	☐ L	Entry	Position Size	☐ TGT ☐ S/L	Execution Score
Setup		☐ S	Exit			

Symbol	Setup Score	☐ L	Entry	Position Size	☐ TGT ☐ S/L	Execution Score
Setup		☐ S	Exit			

Symbol	Setup Score	☐ L	Entry	Position Size	☐ TGT ☐ S/L	Execution Score
Setup		☐ S	Exit			

Symbol	Setup Score	☐ L	Entry	Position Size	☐ TGT ☐ S/L	Execution Score
Setup		☐ S	Exit			

Symbol	Setup Score	☐ L	Entry	Position Size	☐ TGT ☐ S/L	Execution Score
Setup		☐ S	Exit			

Date ☐ Paper ☐ Live

Watchlist

Market Events

Goals & Rewards

Pre-Market Observations

○ ○ ○ ○ ○ ○ ○ ○ ○ ○

Post-Market Observations

☐ 24 Hour Review ☐ End of Week Review ☐ End of Month Review

Symbol	Setup Score	☐ L	Entry	Position Size	☐ TGT ☐ S/L	Execution Score
Setup		☐ S	Exit			

Symbol	Setup Score	☐ L	Entry	Position Size	☐ TGT ☐ S/L	Execution Score
Setup		☐ S	Exit			

Symbol	Setup Score	☐ L	Entry	Position Size	☐ TGT ☐ S/L	Execution Score
Setup		☐ S	Exit			

Symbol	Setup Score	☐ L	Entry	Position Size	☐ TGT ☐ S/L	Execution Score
Setup		☐ S	Exit			

Symbol	Setup Score	☐ L	Entry	Position Size	☐ TGT ☐ S/L	Execution Score
Setup		☐ S	Exit			

Symbol	Setup Score	☐ L	Entry	Position Size	☐ TGT ☐ S/L	Execution Score
Setup		☐ S	Exit			

Symbol	Setup Score	☐ L	Entry	Position Size	☐ TGT ☐ S/L	Execution Score
Setup		☐ S	Exit			

Symbol	Setup Score	☐ L	Entry	Position Size	☐ TGT ☐ S/L	Execution Score
Setup		☐ S	Exit			

Symbol	Setup Score	☐ L	Entry	Position Size	☐ TGT ☐ S/L	Execution Score
Setup		☐ S	Exit			

Symbol	Setup Score	☐ L	Entry	Position Size	☐ TGT ☐ S/L	Execution Score
Setup		☐ S	Exit			

Date | ☐ Paper ☐ Live

Watchlist

Market Events

Goals & Rewards

Pre-Market Observations

○ ○ ○ ○ ○ ○ ○ ○ ○ ○

Post-Market Observations

☐ 24 Hour Review   ☐ End of Week Review   ☐ End of Month Review

Symbol	Setup Score	☐ L	Entry	Position Size	☐ TGT ☐ S/L	Execution Score
Setup		☐ S	Exit			

Symbol	Setup Score	☐ L	Entry	Position Size	☐ TGT ☐ S/L	Execution Score
Setup		☐ S	Exit			

Symbol	Setup Score	☐ L	Entry	Position Size	☐ TGT ☐ S/L	Execution Score
Setup		☐ S	Exit			

Symbol	Setup Score	☐ L	Entry	Position Size	☐ TGT ☐ S/L	Execution Score
Setup		☐ S	Exit			

Symbol	Setup Score	☐ L	Entry	Position Size	☐ TGT ☐ S/L	Execution Score
Setup		☐ S	Exit			

Symbol	Setup Score	☐ L	Entry	Position Size	☐ TGT ☐ S/L	Execution Score
Setup		☐ S	Exit			

Symbol	Setup Score	☐ L	Entry	Position Size	☐ TGT ☐ S/L	Execution Score
Setup		☐ S	Exit			

Symbol	Setup Score	☐ L	Entry	Position Size	☐ TGT ☐ S/L	Execution Score
Setup		☐ S	Exit			

Symbol	Setup Score	☐ L	Entry	Position Size	☐ TGT ☐ S/L	Execution Score
Setup		☐ S	Exit			

Symbol	Setup Score	☐ L	Entry	Position Size	☐ TGT ☐ S/L	Execution Score
Setup		☐ S	Exit			

| Date | ☐ Paper ☐ Live | Watchlist |

Market Events

Goals & Rewards

Pre-Market Observations

○ ○ ○ ○ ○ ○ ○ ○ ○ ○

Post-Market Observations

☐ 24 Hour Review   ☐ End of Week Review   ☐ End of Month Review

Symbol	Setup Score	☐ L	Entry	Position Size	☐ TGT ☐ S/L	Execution Score
Setup		☐ S	Exit			

Symbol	Setup Score	☐ L	Entry	Position Size	☐ TGT ☐ S/L	Execution Score
Setup		☐ S	Exit			

Symbol	Setup Score	☐ L	Entry	Position Size	☐ TGT ☐ S/L	Execution Score
Setup		☐ S	Exit			

Symbol	Setup Score	☐ L	Entry	Position Size	☐ TGT ☐ S/L	Execution Score
Setup		☐ S	Exit			

Symbol	Setup Score	☐ L	Entry	Position Size	☐ TGT ☐ S/L	Execution Score
Setup		☐ S	Exit			

Symbol	Setup Score	☐ L	Entry	Position Size	☐ TGT ☐ S/L	Execution Score
Setup		☐ S	Exit			

Symbol	Setup Score	☐ L	Entry	Position Size	☐ TGT ☐ S/L	Execution Score
Setup		☐ S	Exit			

Symbol	Setup Score	☐ L	Entry	Position Size	☐ TGT ☐ S/L	Execution Score
Setup		☐ S	Exit			

Symbol	Setup Score	☐ L	Entry	Position Size	☐ TGT ☐ S/L	Execution Score
Setup		☐ S	Exit			

Symbol	Setup Score	☐ L	Entry	Position Size	☐ TGT ☐ S/L	Execution Score
Setup		☐ S	Exit			

| Date | ☐ Paper ☐ Live | Watchlist |

Market Events

Goals & Rewards

Pre-Market Observations

○ ○ ○ ○ ○ ○ ○ ○ ○ ○

Post-Market Observations

☐ 24 Hour Review ☐ End of Week Review ☐ End of Month Review

Symbol	Setup Score	☐ L	Entry	Position Size	☐ TGT ☐ S/L	Execution Score
Setup		☐ S	Exit			

Symbol	Setup Score	☐ L	Entry	Position Size	☐ TGT ☐ S/L	Execution Score
Setup		☐ S	Exit			

Symbol	Setup Score	☐ L	Entry	Position Size	☐ TGT ☐ S/L	Execution Score
Setup		☐ S	Exit			

Symbol	Setup Score	☐ L	Entry	Position Size	☐ TGT ☐ S/L	Execution Score
Setup		☐ S	Exit			

Symbol	Setup Score	☐ L	Entry	Position Size	☐ TGT ☐ S/L	Execution Score
Setup		☐ S	Exit			

Symbol	Setup Score	☐ L	Entry	Position Size	☐ TGT ☐ S/L	Execution Score
Setup		☐ S	Exit			

Symbol	Setup Score	☐ L	Entry	Position Size	☐ TGT ☐ S/L	Execution Score
Setup		☐ S	Exit			

Symbol	Setup Score	☐ L	Entry	Position Size	☐ TGT ☐ S/L	Execution Score
Setup		☐ S	Exit			

Symbol	Setup Score	☐ L	Entry	Position Size	☐ TGT ☐ S/L	Execution Score
Setup		☐ S	Exit			

Symbol	Setup Score	☐ L	Entry	Position Size	☐ TGT ☐ S/L	Execution Score
Setup		☐ S	Exit			

| Date | ☐ Paper   ☐ Live | Watchlist |

Market Events

Goals & Rewards

Pre-Market Observations

○ ○ ○ ○ ○ ○ ○ ○ ○ ○

Post-Market Observations

☐ 24 Hour Review   ☐ End of Week Review   ☐ End of Month Review

Symbol	Setup Score	☐ L	Entry	Position Size	☐ TGT ☐ S/L	Execution Score
Setup		☐ S	Exit			

Symbol	Setup Score	☐ L	Entry	Position Size	☐ TGT ☐ S/L	Execution Score
Setup		☐ S	Exit			

Symbol	Setup Score	☐ L	Entry	Position Size	☐ TGT ☐ S/L	Execution Score
Setup		☐ S	Exit			

Symbol	Setup Score	☐ L	Entry	Position Size	☐ TGT ☐ S/L	Execution Score
Setup		☐ S	Exit			

Symbol	Setup Score	☐ L	Entry	Position Size	☐ TGT ☐ S/L	Execution Score
Setup		☐ S	Exit			

Symbol	Setup Score	☐ L	Entry	Position Size	☐ TGT ☐ S/L	Execution Score
Setup		☐ S	Exit			

Symbol	Setup Score	☐ L	Entry	Position Size	☐ TGT ☐ S/L	Execution Score
Setup		☐ S	Exit			

Symbol	Setup Score	☐ L	Entry	Position Size	☐ TGT ☐ S/L	Execution Score
Setup		☐ S	Exit			

Symbol	Setup Score	☐ L	Entry	Position Size	☐ TGT ☐ S/L	Execution Score
Setup		☐ S	Exit			

Symbol	Setup Score	☐ L	Entry	Position Size	☐ TGT ☐ S/L	Execution Score
Setup		☐ S	Exit			

| Date | ☐ Paper   ☐ Live | Watchlist |

Market Events

Goals & Rewards

Pre-Market Observations

◯ ◯ ◯ ◯ ◯ ◯ ◯ ◯ ◯ ◯

Post-Market Observations

☐ 24 Hour Review   ☐ End of Week Review   ☐ End of Month Review

Symbol	Setup Score	☐ L	Entry	Position Size	☐ TGT ☐ S/L	Execution Score
Setup		☐ S	Exit			

Symbol	Setup Score	☐ L	Entry	Position Size	☐ TGT ☐ S/L	Execution Score
Setup		☐ S	Exit			

Symbol	Setup Score	☐ L	Entry	Position Size	☐ TGT ☐ S/L	Execution Score
Setup		☐ S	Exit			

Symbol	Setup Score	☐ L	Entry	Position Size	☐ TGT ☐ S/L	Execution Score
Setup		☐ S	Exit			

Symbol	Setup Score	☐ L	Entry	Position Size	☐ TGT ☐ S/L	Execution Score
Setup		☐ S	Exit			

Symbol	Setup Score	☐ L	Entry	Position Size	☐ TGT ☐ S/L	Execution Score
Setup		☐ S	Exit			

Symbol	Setup Score	☐ L	Entry	Position Size	☐ TGT ☐ S/L	Execution Score
Setup		☐ S	Exit			

Symbol	Setup Score	☐ L	Entry	Position Size	☐ TGT ☐ S/L	Execution Score
Setup		☐ S	Exit			

Symbol	Setup Score	☐ L	Entry	Position Size	☐ TGT ☐ S/L	Execution Score
Setup		☐ S	Exit			

Symbol	Setup Score	☐ L	Entry	Position Size	☐ TGT ☐ S/L	Execution Score
Setup		☐ S	Exit			

| Date | ☐ Paper ☐ Live | Watchlist |

Market Events

Goals & Rewards

Pre-Market Observations

◯ ◯ ◯ ◯ ◯ ◯ ◯ ◯ ◯ ◯ ◯

Post-Market Observations

☐ 24 Hour Review   ☐ End of Week Review   ☐ End of Month Review

Symbol	Setup Score	☐ L	Entry	Position Size	☐ TGT ☐ S/L	Execution Score
Setup		☐ S	Exit			

Symbol	Setup Score	☐ L	Entry	Position Size	☐ TGT ☐ S/L	Execution Score
Setup		☐ S	Exit			

Symbol	Setup Score	☐ L	Entry	Position Size	☐ TGT ☐ S/L	Execution Score
Setup		☐ S	Exit			

Symbol	Setup Score	☐ L	Entry	Position Size	☐ TGT ☐ S/L	Execution Score
Setup		☐ S	Exit			

Symbol	Setup Score	☐ L	Entry	Position Size	☐ TGT ☐ S/L	Execution Score
Setup		☐ S	Exit			

Symbol	Setup Score	☐ L	Entry	Position Size	☐ TGT ☐ S/L	Execution Score
Setup		☐ S	Exit			

Symbol	Setup Score	☐ L	Entry	Position Size	☐ TGT ☐ S/L	Execution Score
Setup		☐ S	Exit			

Symbol	Setup Score	☐ L	Entry	Position Size	☐ TGT ☐ S/L	Execution Score
Setup		☐ S	Exit			

Symbol	Setup Score	☐ L	Entry	Position Size	☐ TGT ☐ S/L	Execution Score
Setup		☐ S	Exit			

Symbol	Setup Score	☐ L	Entry	Position Size	☐ TGT ☐ S/L	Execution Score
Setup		☐ S	Exit			

| Date | ☐ Paper ☐ Live | Watchlist |

Market Events

Goals & Rewards

Pre-Market Observations

○ ○ ○ ○ ○ ○ ○ ○ ○ ○ ○

Post-Market Observations

☐ 24 Hour Review   ☐ End of Week Review   ☐ End of Month Review

Symbol	Setup Score	☐ L	Entry	Position Size	☐ TGT ☐ S/L	Execution Score
Setup		☐ S	Exit			

Symbol	Setup Score	☐ L	Entry	Position Size	☐ TGT ☐ S/L	Execution Score
Setup		☐ S	Exit			

Symbol	Setup Score	☐ L	Entry	Position Size	☐ TGT ☐ S/L	Execution Score
Setup		☐ S	Exit			

Symbol	Setup Score	☐ L	Entry	Position Size	☐ TGT ☐ S/L	Execution Score
Setup		☐ S	Exit			

Symbol	Setup Score	☐ L	Entry	Position Size	☐ TGT ☐ S/L	Execution Score
Setup		☐ S	Exit			

Symbol	Setup Score	☐ L	Entry	Position Size	☐ TGT ☐ S/L	Execution Score
Setup		☐ S	Exit			

Symbol	Setup Score	☐ L	Entry	Position Size	☐ TGT ☐ S/L	Execution Score
Setup		☐ S	Exit			

Symbol	Setup Score	☐ L	Entry	Position Size	☐ TGT ☐ S/L	Execution Score
Setup		☐ S	Exit			

Symbol	Setup Score	☐ L	Entry	Position Size	☐ TGT ☐ S/L	Execution Score
Setup		☐ S	Exit			

Symbol	Setup Score	☐ L	Entry	Position Size	☐ TGT ☐ S/L	Execution Score
Setup		☐ S	Exit			

Date ☐ Paper ☐ Live

Watchlist

Market Events

Goals & Rewards

Pre-Market Observations

○ ○ ○ ○ ○ ○ ○ ○ ○ ○ ○

Post-Market Observations

☐ 24 Hour Review ☐ End of Week Review ☐ End of Month Review

Symbol	Setup Score	☐ L	Entry	Position Size	☐ TGT ☐ S/L	Execution Score
Setup		☐ S	Exit			

Symbol	Setup Score	☐ L	Entry	Position Size	☐ TGT ☐ S/L	Execution Score
Setup		☐ S	Exit			

Symbol	Setup Score	☐ L	Entry	Position Size	☐ TGT ☐ S/L	Execution Score
Setup		☐ S	Exit			

Symbol	Setup Score	☐ L	Entry	Position Size	☐ TGT ☐ S/L	Execution Score
Setup		☐ S	Exit			

Symbol	Setup Score	☐ L	Entry	Position Size	☐ TGT ☐ S/L	Execution Score
Setup		☐ S	Exit			

Symbol	Setup Score	☐ L	Entry	Position Size	☐ TGT ☐ S/L	Execution Score
Setup		☐ S	Exit			

Symbol	Setup Score	☐ L	Entry	Position Size	☐ TGT ☐ S/L	Execution Score
Setup		☐ S	Exit			

Symbol	Setup Score	☐ L	Entry	Position Size	☐ TGT ☐ S/L	Execution Score
Setup		☐ S	Exit			

Symbol	Setup Score	☐ L	Entry	Position Size	☐ TGT ☐ S/L	Execution Score
Setup		☐ S	Exit			

Symbol	Setup Score	☐ L	Entry	Position Size	☐ TGT ☐ S/L	Execution Score
Setup		☐ S	Exit			

| Date | ☐ Paper ☐ Live | Watchlist |

Market Events

Goals & Rewards

Pre-Market Observations

○ ○ ○ ○ ○ ○ ○ ○ ○ ○ ○

Post-Market Observations

☐ 24 Hour Review ☐ End of Week Review ☐ End of Month Review

Symbol	Setup Score	☐ L	Entry	Position Size	☐ TGT ☐ S/L	Execution Score
Setup		☐ S	Exit			

Symbol	Setup Score	☐ L	Entry	Position Size	☐ TGT ☐ S/L	Execution Score
Setup		☐ S	Exit			

Symbol	Setup Score	☐ L	Entry	Position Size	☐ TGT ☐ S/L	Execution Score
Setup		☐ S	Exit			

Symbol	Setup Score	☐ L	Entry	Position Size	☐ TGT ☐ S/L	Execution Score
Setup		☐ S	Exit			

Symbol	Setup Score	☐ L	Entry	Position Size	☐ TGT ☐ S/L	Execution Score
Setup		☐ S	Exit			

Symbol	Setup Score	☐ L	Entry	Position Size	☐ TGT ☐ S/L	Execution Score
Setup		☐ S	Exit			

Symbol	Setup Score	☐ L	Entry	Position Size	☐ TGT ☐ S/L	Execution Score
Setup		☐ S	Exit			

Symbol	Setup Score	☐ L	Entry	Position Size	☐ TGT ☐ S/L	Execution Score
Setup		☐ S	Exit			

Symbol	Setup Score	☐ L	Entry	Position Size	☐ TGT ☐ S/L	Execution Score
Setup		☐ S	Exit			

Symbol	Setup Score	☐ L	Entry	Position Size	☐ TGT ☐ S/L	Execution Score
Setup		☐ S	Exit			

Date ☐ Paper ☐ Live

Watchlist

Market Events

Goals & Rewards

Pre-Market Observations

○ ○ ○ ○ ○ ○ ○ ○ ○ ○

Post-Market Observations

☐ 24 Hour Review ☐ End of Week Review ☐ End of Month Review

Symbol	Setup Score	☐ L	Entry	Position Size	☐ TGT ☐ S/L	Execution Score
Setup		☐ S	Exit			

Symbol	Setup Score	☐ L	Entry	Position Size	☐ TGT ☐ S/L	Execution Score
Setup		☐ S	Exit			

Symbol	Setup Score	☐ L	Entry	Position Size	☐ TGT ☐ S/L	Execution Score
Setup		☐ S	Exit			

Symbol	Setup Score	☐ L	Entry	Position Size	☐ TGT ☐ S/L	Execution Score
Setup		☐ S	Exit			

Symbol	Setup Score	☐ L	Entry	Position Size	☐ TGT ☐ S/L	Execution Score
Setup		☐ S	Exit			

Symbol	Setup Score	☐ L	Entry	Position Size	☐ TGT ☐ S/L	Execution Score
Setup		☐ S	Exit			

Symbol	Setup Score	☐ L	Entry	Position Size	☐ TGT ☐ S/L	Execution Score
Setup		☐ S	Exit			

Symbol	Setup Score	☐ L	Entry	Position Size	☐ TGT ☐ S/L	Execution Score
Setup		☐ S	Exit			

Symbol	Setup Score	☐ L	Entry	Position Size	☐ TGT ☐ S/L	Execution Score
Setup		☐ S	Exit			

Symbol	Setup Score	☐ L	Entry	Position Size	☐ TGT ☐ S/L	Execution Score
Setup		☐ S	Exit			

Date ☐ Paper ☐ Live

Watchlist

Market Events

Goals & Rewards

Pre-Market Observations

○ ○ ○ ○ ○ ○ ○ ○ ○ ○

Post-Market Observations

☐ 24 Hour Review   ☐ End of Week Review   ☐ End of Month Review

Symbol	Setup Score	☐ L	Entry	Position Size	☐ TGT ☐ S/L	Execution Score
Setup		☐ S	Exit			

Symbol	Setup Score	☐ L	Entry	Position Size	☐ TGT ☐ S/L	Execution Score
Setup		☐ S	Exit			

Symbol	Setup Score	☐ L	Entry	Position Size	☐ TGT ☐ S/L	Execution Score
Setup		☐ S	Exit			

Symbol	Setup Score	☐ L	Entry	Position Size	☐ TGT ☐ S/L	Execution Score
Setup		☐ S	Exit			

Symbol	Setup Score	☐ L	Entry	Position Size	☐ TGT ☐ S/L	Execution Score
Setup		☐ S	Exit			

Symbol	Setup Score	☐ L	Entry	Position Size	☐ TGT ☐ S/L	Execution Score
Setup		☐ S	Exit			

Symbol	Setup Score	☐ L	Entry	Position Size	☐ TGT ☐ S/L	Execution Score
Setup		☐ S	Exit			

Symbol	Setup Score	☐ L	Entry	Position Size	☐ TGT ☐ S/L	Execution Score
Setup		☐ S	Exit			

Symbol	Setup Score	☐ L	Entry	Position Size	☐ TGT ☐ S/L	Execution Score
Setup		☐ S	Exit			

Symbol	Setup Score	☐ L	Entry	Position Size	☐ TGT ☐ S/L	Execution Score
Setup		☐ S	Exit			

| Date | ☐ Paper ☐ Live | Watchlist |

Market Events

Goals & Rewards

Pre-Market Observations

○ ○ ○ ○ ○ ○ ○ ○ ○ ○

Post-Market Observations

☐ 24 Hour Review   ☐ End of Week Review   ☐ End of Month Review

Symbol	Setup Score	☐ L	Entry	Position Size	☐ TGT ☐ S/L	Execution Score
Setup		☐ S	Exit			

Symbol	Setup Score	☐ L	Entry	Position Size	☐ TGT ☐ S/L	Execution Score
Setup		☐ S	Exit			

Symbol	Setup Score	☐ L	Entry	Position Size	☐ TGT ☐ S/L	Execution Score
Setup		☐ S	Exit			

Symbol	Setup Score	☐ L	Entry	Position Size	☐ TGT ☐ S/L	Execution Score
Setup		☐ S	Exit			

Symbol	Setup Score	☐ L	Entry	Position Size	☐ TGT ☐ S/L	Execution Score
Setup		☐ S	Exit			

Symbol	Setup Score	☐ L	Entry	Position Size	☐ TGT ☐ S/L	Execution Score
Setup		☐ S	Exit			

Symbol	Setup Score	☐ L	Entry	Position Size	☐ TGT ☐ S/L	Execution Score
Setup		☐ S	Exit			

Symbol	Setup Score	☐ L	Entry	Position Size	☐ TGT ☐ S/L	Execution Score
Setup		☐ S	Exit			

Symbol	Setup Score	☐ L	Entry	Position Size	☐ TGT ☐ S/L	Execution Score
Setup		☐ S	Exit			

Symbol	Setup Score	☐ L	Entry	Position Size	☐ TGT ☐ S/L	Execution Score
Setup		☐ S	Exit			

Date ☐ Paper ☐ Live

Watchlist

Market Events

Goals & Rewards

Pre-Market Observations

○ ○ ○ ○ ○ ○ ○ ○ ○ ○

Post-Market Observations

☐ 24 Hour Review ☐ End of Week Review ☐ End of Month Review

Symbol	Setup Score	☐ L	Entry	Position Size	☐ TGT ☐ S/L	Execution Score
Setup		☐ S	Exit			

Symbol	Setup Score	☐ L	Entry	Position Size	☐ TGT ☐ S/L	Execution Score
Setup		☐ S	Exit			

Symbol	Setup Score	☐ L	Entry	Position Size	☐ TGT ☐ S/L	Execution Score
Setup		☐ S	Exit			

Symbol	Setup Score	☐ L	Entry	Position Size	☐ TGT ☐ S/L	Execution Score
Setup		☐ S	Exit			

Symbol	Setup Score	☐ L	Entry	Position Size	☐ TGT ☐ S/L	Execution Score
Setup		☐ S	Exit			

Symbol	Setup Score	☐ L	Entry	Position Size	☐ TGT ☐ S/L	Execution Score
Setup		☐ S	Exit			

Symbol	Setup Score	☐ L	Entry	Position Size	☐ TGT ☐ S/L	Execution Score
Setup		☐ S	Exit			

Symbol	Setup Score	☐ L	Entry	Position Size	☐ TGT ☐ S/L	Execution Score
Setup		☐ S	Exit			

Symbol	Setup Score	☐ L	Entry	Position Size	☐ TGT ☐ S/L	Execution Score
Setup		☐ S	Exit			

Symbol	Setup Score	☐ L	Entry	Position Size	☐ TGT ☐ S/L	Execution Score
Setup		☐ S	Exit			

Date ☐ Paper ☐ Live

Watchlist

Market Events

Goals & Rewards

Pre-Market Observations

○ ○ ○ ○ ○ ○ ○ ○ ○ ○ ○

Post-Market Observations

☐ 24 Hour Review   ☐ End of Week Review   ☐ End of Month Review

Symbol	Setup Score	☐ L	Entry	Position Size	☐ TGT ☐ S/L	Execution Score
Setup		☐ S	Exit			

Symbol	Setup Score	☐ L	Entry	Position Size	☐ TGT ☐ S/L	Execution Score
Setup		☐ S	Exit			

Symbol	Setup Score	☐ L	Entry	Position Size	☐ TGT ☐ S/L	Execution Score
Setup		☐ S	Exit			

Symbol	Setup Score	☐ L	Entry	Position Size	☐ TGT ☐ S/L	Execution Score
Setup		☐ S	Exit			

Symbol	Setup Score	☐ L	Entry	Position Size	☐ TGT ☐ S/L	Execution Score
Setup		☐ S	Exit			

Symbol	Setup Score	☐ L	Entry	Position Size	☐ TGT ☐ S/L	Execution Score
Setup		☐ S	Exit			

Symbol	Setup Score	☐ L	Entry	Position Size	☐ TGT ☐ S/L	Execution Score
Setup		☐ S	Exit			

Symbol	Setup Score	☐ L	Entry	Position Size	☐ TGT ☐ S/L	Execution Score
Setup		☐ S	Exit			

Symbol	Setup Score	☐ L	Entry	Position Size	☐ TGT ☐ S/L	Execution Score
Setup		☐ S	Exit			

Symbol	Setup Score	☐ L	Entry	Position Size	☐ TGT ☐ S/L	Execution Score
Setup		☐ S	Exit			

| Date | ☐ Paper ☐ Live | Watchlist |

Market Events

Goals & Rewards

Pre-Market Observations

○ ○ ○ ○ ○ ○ ○ ○ ○ ○

Post-Market Observations

☐ 24 Hour Review   ☐ End of Week Review   ☐ End of Month Review

Symbol	Setup Score	☐ L	Entry	Position Size	☐ TGT ☐ S/L	Execution Score
Setup		☐ S	Exit			

Symbol	Setup Score	☐ L	Entry	Position Size	☐ TGT ☐ S/L	Execution Score
Setup		☐ S	Exit			

Symbol	Setup Score	☐ L	Entry	Position Size	☐ TGT ☐ S/L	Execution Score
Setup		☐ S	Exit			

Symbol	Setup Score	☐ L	Entry	Position Size	☐ TGT ☐ S/L	Execution Score
Setup		☐ S	Exit			

Symbol	Setup Score	☐ L	Entry	Position Size	☐ TGT ☐ S/L	Execution Score
Setup		☐ S	Exit			

Symbol	Setup Score	☐ L	Entry	Position Size	☐ TGT ☐ S/L	Execution Score
Setup		☐ S	Exit			

Symbol	Setup Score	☐ L	Entry	Position Size	☐ TGT ☐ S/L	Execution Score
Setup		☐ S	Exit			

Symbol	Setup Score	☐ L	Entry	Position Size	☐ TGT ☐ S/L	Execution Score
Setup		☐ S	Exit			

Symbol	Setup Score	☐ L	Entry	Position Size	☐ TGT ☐ S/L	Execution Score
Setup		☐ S	Exit			

Symbol	Setup Score	☐ L	Entry	Position Size	☐ TGT ☐ S/L	Execution Score
Setup		☐ S	Exit			

Date ☐ Paper ☐ Live

Watchlist

Market Events

Goals & Rewards

Pre-Market Observations

Post-Market Observations

☐ 24 Hour Review   ☐ End of Week Review   ☐ End of Month Review

Symbol	Setup Score	☐ L	Entry	Position Size	☐ TGT ☐ S/L	Execution Score
Setup		☐ S	Exit			

Symbol	Setup Score	☐ L	Entry	Position Size	☐ TGT ☐ S/L	Execution Score
Setup		☐ S	Exit			

Symbol	Setup Score	☐ L	Entry	Position Size	☐ TGT ☐ S/L	Execution Score
Setup		☐ S	Exit			

Symbol	Setup Score	☐ L	Entry	Position Size	☐ TGT ☐ S/L	Execution Score
Setup		☐ S	Exit			

Symbol	Setup Score	☐ L	Entry	Position Size	☐ TGT ☐ S/L	Execution Score
Setup		☐ S	Exit			

Symbol	Setup Score	☐ L	Entry	Position Size	☐ TGT ☐ S/L	Execution Score
Setup		☐ S	Exit			

Symbol	Setup Score	☐ L	Entry	Position Size	☐ TGT ☐ S/L	Execution Score
Setup		☐ S	Exit			

Symbol	Setup Score	☐ L	Entry	Position Size	☐ TGT ☐ S/L	Execution Score
Setup		☐ S	Exit			

Symbol	Setup Score	☐ L	Entry	Position Size	☐ TGT ☐ S/L	Execution Score
Setup		☐ S	Exit			

Symbol	Setup Score	☐ L	Entry	Position Size	☐ TGT ☐ S/L	Execution Score
Setup		☐ S	Exit			

| Date | ☐ Paper ☐ Live | Watchlist |

Market Events

Goals & Rewards

Pre-Market Observations

○ ○ ○ ○ ○ ○ ○ ○ ○ ○

Post-Market Observations

☐ 24 Hour Review ☐ End of Week Review ☐ End of Month Review

Symbol		Setup Score	☐ L	Entry		Position Size	☐ TGT ☐ S/L	Execution Score
Setup			☐ S	Exit				

Symbol		Setup Score	☐ L	Entry		Position Size	☐ TGT ☐ S/L	Execution Score
Setup			☐ S	Exit				

Symbol		Setup Score	☐ L	Entry		Position Size	☐ TGT ☐ S/L	Execution Score
Setup			☐ S	Exit				

Symbol		Setup Score	☐ L	Entry		Position Size	☐ TGT ☐ S/L	Execution Score
Setup			☐ S	Exit				

Symbol		Setup Score	☐ L	Entry		Position Size	☐ TGT ☐ S/L	Execution Score
Setup			☐ S	Exit				

Symbol		Setup Score	☐ L	Entry		Position Size	☐ TGT ☐ S/L	Execution Score
Setup			☐ S	Exit				

Symbol		Setup Score	☐ L	Entry		Position Size	☐ TGT ☐ S/L	Execution Score
Setup			☐ S	Exit				

Symbol		Setup Score	☐ L	Entry		Position Size	☐ TGT ☐ S/L	Execution Score
Setup			☐ S	Exit				

Symbol		Setup Score	☐ L	Entry		Position Size	☐ TGT ☐ S/L	Execution Score
Setup			☐ S	Exit				

Symbol		Setup Score	☐ L	Entry		Position Size	☐ TGT ☐ S/L	Execution Score
Setup			☐ S	Exit				

| Date | ☐ Paper ☐ Live | Watchlist |

Market Events

Goals & Rewards

Pre-Market Observations

○ ○ ○ ○ ○ ○ ○ ○ ○ ○

Post-Market Observations

☐ 24 Hour Review ☐ End of Week Review ☐ End of Month Review

Symbol		Setup Score	☐ L	Entry		Position Size	☐ TGT ☐ S/L	Execution Score
Setup			☐ S	Exit				

Symbol		Setup Score	☐ L	Entry		Position Size	☐ TGT ☐ S/L	Execution Score
Setup			☐ S	Exit				

Symbol		Setup Score	☐ L	Entry		Position Size	☐ TGT ☐ S/L	Execution Score
Setup			☐ S	Exit				

Symbol		Setup Score	☐ L	Entry		Position Size	☐ TGT ☐ S/L	Execution Score
Setup			☐ S	Exit				

Symbol		Setup Score	☐ L	Entry		Position Size	☐ TGT ☐ S/L	Execution Score
Setup			☐ S	Exit				

Symbol		Setup Score	☐ L	Entry		Position Size	☐ TGT ☐ S/L	Execution Score
Setup			☐ S	Exit				

Symbol		Setup Score	☐ L	Entry		Position Size	☐ TGT ☐ S/L	Execution Score
Setup			☐ S	Exit				

Symbol		Setup Score	☐ L	Entry		Position Size	☐ TGT ☐ S/L	Execution Score
Setup			☐ S	Exit				

Symbol		Setup Score	☐ L	Entry		Position Size	☐ TGT ☐ S/L	Execution Score
Setup			☐ S	Exit				

Symbol		Setup Score	☐ L	Entry		Position Size	☐ TGT ☐ S/L	Execution Score
Setup			☐ S	Exit				

| Date | ☐ Paper   ☐ Live | Watchlist |

Market Events

Goals & Rewards

Pre-Market Observations

○ ○ ○ ○ ○ ○ ○ ○ ○ ○

Post-Market Observations

☐ 24 Hour Review   ☐ End of Week Review   ☐ End of Month Review

Symbol	Setup Score	☐ L	Entry	Position Size	☐ TGT ☐ S/L	Execution Score
Setup		☐ S	Exit			

Symbol	Setup Score	☐ L	Entry	Position Size	☐ TGT ☐ S/L	Execution Score
Setup		☐ S	Exit			

Symbol	Setup Score	☐ L	Entry	Position Size	☐ TGT ☐ S/L	Execution Score
Setup		☐ S	Exit			

Symbol	Setup Score	☐ L	Entry	Position Size	☐ TGT ☐ S/L	Execution Score
Setup		☐ S	Exit			

Symbol	Setup Score	☐ L	Entry	Position Size	☐ TGT ☐ S/L	Execution Score
Setup		☐ S	Exit			

Symbol	Setup Score	☐ L	Entry	Position Size	☐ TGT ☐ S/L	Execution Score
Setup		☐ S	Exit			

Symbol	Setup Score	☐ L	Entry	Position Size	☐ TGT ☐ S/L	Execution Score
Setup		☐ S	Exit			

Symbol	Setup Score	☐ L	Entry	Position Size	☐ TGT ☐ S/L	Execution Score
Setup		☐ S	Exit			

Symbol	Setup Score	☐ L	Entry	Position Size	☐ TGT ☐ S/L	Execution Score
Setup		☐ S	Exit			

Symbol	Setup Score	☐ L	Entry	Position Size	☐ TGT ☐ S/L	Execution Score
Setup		☐ S	Exit			

Date	☐ Paper ☐ Live	Watchlist

Market Events

Goals & Rewards

Pre-Market Observations

○ ○ ○ ○ ○ ○ ○ ○ ○ ○ ○

Post-Market Observations

☐ 24 Hour Review   ☐ End of Week Review   ☐ End of Month Review

Symbol	Setup Score	☐ L	Entry	Position Size	☐ TGT ☐ S/L	Execution Score
Setup		☐ S	Exit			

Symbol	Setup Score	☐ L	Entry	Position Size	☐ TGT ☐ S/L	Execution Score
Setup		☐ S	Exit			

Symbol	Setup Score	☐ L	Entry	Position Size	☐ TGT ☐ S/L	Execution Score
Setup		☐ S	Exit			

Symbol	Setup Score	☐ L	Entry	Position Size	☐ TGT ☐ S/L	Execution Score
Setup		☐ S	Exit			

Symbol	Setup Score	☐ L	Entry	Position Size	☐ TGT ☐ S/L	Execution Score
Setup		☐ S	Exit			

Symbol	Setup Score	☐ L	Entry	Position Size	☐ TGT ☐ S/L	Execution Score
Setup		☐ S	Exit			

Symbol	Setup Score	☐ L	Entry	Position Size	☐ TGT ☐ S/L	Execution Score
Setup		☐ S	Exit			

Symbol	Setup Score	☐ L	Entry	Position Size	☐ TGT ☐ S/L	Execution Score
Setup		☐ S	Exit			

Symbol	Setup Score	☐ L	Entry	Position Size	☐ TGT ☐ S/L	Execution Score
Setup		☐ S	Exit			

Symbol	Setup Score	☐ L	Entry	Position Size	☐ TGT ☐ S/L	Execution Score
Setup		☐ S	Exit			

| Date | ☐ Paper ☐ Live | Watchlist |

Market Events

Goals & Rewards

Pre-Market Observations

○ ○ ○ ○ ○ ○ ○ ○ ○ ○

Post-Market Observations

☐ 24 Hour Review   ☐ End of Week Review   ☐ End of Month Review

Symbol	Setup Score	☐ L	Entry	Position Size	☐ TGT ☐ S/L	Execution Score
Setup		☐ S	Exit			

Symbol	Setup Score	☐ L	Entry	Position Size	☐ TGT ☐ S/L	Execution Score
Setup		☐ S	Exit			

Symbol	Setup Score	☐ L	Entry	Position Size	☐ TGT ☐ S/L	Execution Score
Setup		☐ S	Exit			

Symbol	Setup Score	☐ L	Entry	Position Size	☐ TGT ☐ S/L	Execution Score
Setup		☐ S	Exit			

Symbol	Setup Score	☐ L	Entry	Position Size	☐ TGT ☐ S/L	Execution Score
Setup		☐ S	Exit			

Symbol	Setup Score	☐ L	Entry	Position Size	☐ TGT ☐ S/L	Execution Score
Setup		☐ S	Exit			

Symbol	Setup Score	☐ L	Entry	Position Size	☐ TGT ☐ S/L	Execution Score
Setup		☐ S	Exit			

Symbol	Setup Score	☐ L	Entry	Position Size	☐ TGT ☐ S/L	Execution Score
Setup		☐ S	Exit			

Symbol	Setup Score	☐ L	Entry	Position Size	☐ TGT ☐ S/L	Execution Score
Setup		☐ S	Exit			

Symbol	Setup Score	☐ L	Entry	Position Size	☐ TGT ☐ S/L	Execution Score
Setup		☐ S	Exit			

| Date | ☐ Paper ☐ Live | Watchlist |

Market Events

Goals & Rewards

Pre-Market Observations

◯ ◯ ◯ ◯ ◯ ◯ ◯ ◯ ◯ ◯ ◯

Post-Market Observations

☐ 24 Hour Review ☐ End of Week Review ☐ End of Month Review

Symbol	Setup Score	☐ L	Entry	Position Size	☐ TGT ☐ S/L	Execution Score
Setup		☐ S	Exit			

Symbol	Setup Score	☐ L	Entry	Position Size	☐ TGT ☐ S/L	Execution Score
Setup		☐ S	Exit			

Symbol	Setup Score	☐ L	Entry	Position Size	☐ TGT ☐ S/L	Execution Score
Setup		☐ S	Exit			

Symbol	Setup Score	☐ L	Entry	Position Size	☐ TGT ☐ S/L	Execution Score
Setup		☐ S	Exit			

Symbol	Setup Score	☐ L	Entry	Position Size	☐ TGT ☐ S/L	Execution Score
Setup		☐ S	Exit			

Symbol	Setup Score	☐ L	Entry	Position Size	☐ TGT ☐ S/L	Execution Score
Setup		☐ S	Exit			

Symbol	Setup Score	☐ L	Entry	Position Size	☐ TGT ☐ S/L	Execution Score
Setup		☐ S	Exit			

Symbol	Setup Score	☐ L	Entry	Position Size	☐ TGT ☐ S/L	Execution Score
Setup		☐ S	Exit			

Symbol	Setup Score	☐ L	Entry	Position Size	☐ TGT ☐ S/L	Execution Score
Setup		☐ S	Exit			

Symbol	Setup Score	☐ L	Entry	Position Size	☐ TGT ☐ S/L	Execution Score
Setup		☐ S	Exit			

| Date | ☐ Paper   ☐ Live | Watchlist |

Market Events

Goals & Rewards

Pre-Market Observations

○ ○ ○ ○ ○ ○ ○ ○ ○ ○ ○

Post-Market Observations

☐ 24 Hour Review   ☐ End of Week Review   ☐ End of Month Review

Symbol	Setup Score	☐ L	Entry	Position Size	☐ TGT ☐ S/L	Execution Score
Setup		☐ S	Exit			

Symbol	Setup Score	☐ L	Entry	Position Size	☐ TGT ☐ S/L	Execution Score
Setup		☐ S	Exit			

Symbol	Setup Score	☐ L	Entry	Position Size	☐ TGT ☐ S/L	Execution Score
Setup		☐ S	Exit			

Symbol	Setup Score	☐ L	Entry	Position Size	☐ TGT ☐ S/L	Execution Score
Setup		☐ S	Exit			

Symbol	Setup Score	☐ L	Entry	Position Size	☐ TGT ☐ S/L	Execution Score
Setup		☐ S	Exit			

Symbol	Setup Score	☐ L	Entry	Position Size	☐ TGT ☐ S/L	Execution Score
Setup		☐ S	Exit			

Symbol	Setup Score	☐ L	Entry	Position Size	☐ TGT ☐ S/L	Execution Score
Setup		☐ S	Exit			

Symbol	Setup Score	☐ L	Entry	Position Size	☐ TGT ☐ S/L	Execution Score
Setup		☐ S	Exit			

Symbol	Setup Score	☐ L	Entry	Position Size	☐ TGT ☐ S/L	Execution Score
Setup		☐ S	Exit			

Symbol	Setup Score	☐ L	Entry	Position Size	☐ TGT ☐ S/L	Execution Score
Setup		☐ S	Exit			

| Date | ☐ Paper ☐ Live | Watchlist |

Market Events

Goals & Rewards

Pre-Market Observations

○ ○ ○ ○ ○ ○ ○ ○ ○ ○

Post-Market Observations

☐ 24 Hour Review   ☐ End of Week Review   ☐ End of Month Review

Symbol	Setup Score	☐ L	Entry	Position Size	☐ TGT ☐ S/L	Execution Score
Setup		☐ S	Exit			

Symbol	Setup Score	☐ L	Entry	Position Size	☐ TGT ☐ S/L	Execution Score
Setup		☐ S	Exit			

Symbol	Setup Score	☐ L	Entry	Position Size	☐ TGT ☐ S/L	Execution Score
Setup		☐ S	Exit			

Symbol	Setup Score	☐ L	Entry	Position Size	☐ TGT ☐ S/L	Execution Score
Setup		☐ S	Exit			

Symbol	Setup Score	☐ L	Entry	Position Size	☐ TGT ☐ S/L	Execution Score
Setup		☐ S	Exit			

Symbol	Setup Score	☐ L	Entry	Position Size	☐ TGT ☐ S/L	Execution Score
Setup		☐ S	Exit			

Symbol	Setup Score	☐ L	Entry	Position Size	☐ TGT ☐ S/L	Execution Score
Setup		☐ S	Exit			

Symbol	Setup Score	☐ L	Entry	Position Size	☐ TGT ☐ S/L	Execution Score
Setup		☐ S	Exit			

Symbol	Setup Score	☐ L	Entry	Position Size	☐ TGT ☐ S/L	Execution Score
Setup		☐ S	Exit			

Symbol	Setup Score	☐ L	Entry	Position Size	☐ TGT ☐ S/L	Execution Score
Setup		☐ S	Exit			

| Date | ☐ Paper ☐ Live | Watchlist |

Market Events

Goals & Rewards

Pre-Market Observations

○ ○ ○ ○ ○ ○ ○ ○ ○ ○

Post-Market Observations

☐ 24 Hour Review   ☐ End of Week Review   ☐ End of Month Review

Symbol	Setup Score	☐ L	Entry	Position Size	☐ TGT ☐ S/L	Execution Score
Setup		☐ S	Exit			

Symbol	Setup Score	☐ L	Entry	Position Size	☐ TGT ☐ S/L	Execution Score
Setup		☐ S	Exit			

Symbol	Setup Score	☐ L	Entry	Position Size	☐ TGT ☐ S/L	Execution Score
Setup		☐ S	Exit			

Symbol	Setup Score	☐ L	Entry	Position Size	☐ TGT ☐ S/L	Execution Score
Setup		☐ S	Exit			

Symbol	Setup Score	☐ L	Entry	Position Size	☐ TGT ☐ S/L	Execution Score
Setup		☐ S	Exit			

Symbol	Setup Score	☐ L	Entry	Position Size	☐ TGT ☐ S/L	Execution Score
Setup		☐ S	Exit			

Symbol	Setup Score	☐ L	Entry	Position Size	☐ TGT ☐ S/L	Execution Score
Setup		☐ S	Exit			

Symbol	Setup Score	☐ L	Entry	Position Size	☐ TGT ☐ S/L	Execution Score
Setup		☐ S	Exit			

Symbol	Setup Score	☐ L	Entry	Position Size	☐ TGT ☐ S/L	Execution Score
Setup		☐ S	Exit			

Symbol	Setup Score	☐ L	Entry	Position Size	☐ TGT ☐ S/L	Execution Score
Setup		☐ S	Exit			

| Date | ☐ Paper ☐ Live | Watchlist |

Market Events

Goals & Rewards

Pre-Market Observations

◯ ◯ ◯ ◯ ◯ ◯ ◯ ◯ ◯ ◯

Post-Market Observations

☐ 24 Hour Review   ☐ End of Week Review   ☐ End of Month Review

Symbol	Setup Score	☐ L	Entry	Position Size	☐ TGT ☐ S/L	Execution Score
Setup		☐ S	Exit			

Symbol	Setup Score	☐ L	Entry	Position Size	☐ TGT ☐ S/L	Execution Score
Setup		☐ S	Exit			

Symbol	Setup Score	☐ L	Entry	Position Size	☐ TGT ☐ S/L	Execution Score
Setup		☐ S	Exit			

Symbol	Setup Score	☐ L	Entry	Position Size	☐ TGT ☐ S/L	Execution Score
Setup		☐ S	Exit			

Symbol	Setup Score	☐ L	Entry	Position Size	☐ TGT ☐ S/L	Execution Score
Setup		☐ S	Exit			

Symbol	Setup Score	☐ L	Entry	Position Size	☐ TGT ☐ S/L	Execution Score
Setup		☐ S	Exit			

Symbol	Setup Score	☐ L	Entry	Position Size	☐ TGT ☐ S/L	Execution Score
Setup		☐ S	Exit			

Symbol	Setup Score	☐ L	Entry	Position Size	☐ TGT ☐ S/L	Execution Score
Setup		☐ S	Exit			

Symbol	Setup Score	☐ L	Entry	Position Size	☐ TGT ☐ S/L	Execution Score
Setup		☐ S	Exit			

Symbol	Setup Score	☐ L	Entry	Position Size	☐ TGT ☐ S/L	Execution Score
Setup		☐ S	Exit			

Date	☐ Paper ☐ Live	Watchlist

Market Events

Goals & Rewards

Pre-Market Observations

○ ○ ○ ○ ○ ○ ○ ○ ○ ○

Post-Market Observations

☐ 24 Hour Review   ☐ End of Week Review   ☐ End of Month Review

Symbol	Setup Score	☐ L	Entry	Position Size	☐ TGT ☐ S/L	Execution Score
Setup		☐ S	Exit			

Symbol	Setup Score	☐ L	Entry	Position Size	☐ TGT ☐ S/L	Execution Score
Setup		☐ S	Exit			

Symbol	Setup Score	☐ L	Entry	Position Size	☐ TGT ☐ S/L	Execution Score
Setup		☐ S	Exit			

Symbol	Setup Score	☐ L	Entry	Position Size	☐ TGT ☐ S/L	Execution Score
Setup		☐ S	Exit			

Symbol	Setup Score	☐ L	Entry	Position Size	☐ TGT ☐ S/L	Execution Score
Setup		☐ S	Exit			

Symbol	Setup Score	☐ L	Entry	Position Size	☐ TGT ☐ S/L	Execution Score
Setup		☐ S	Exit			

Symbol	Setup Score	☐ L	Entry	Position Size	☐ TGT ☐ S/L	Execution Score
Setup		☐ S	Exit			

Symbol	Setup Score	☐ L	Entry	Position Size	☐ TGT ☐ S/L	Execution Score
Setup		☐ S	Exit			

Symbol	Setup Score	☐ L	Entry	Position Size	☐ TGT ☐ S/L	Execution Score
Setup		☐ S	Exit			

Symbol	Setup Score	☐ L	Entry	Position Size	☐ TGT ☐ S/L	Execution Score
Setup		☐ S	Exit			

| Date | ☐ Paper ☐ Live | Watchlist |

Market Events

Goals & Rewards

Pre-Market Observations

◯ ◯ ◯ ◯ ◯ ◯ ◯ ◯ ◯ ◯

Post-Market Observations

☐ 24 Hour Review   ☐ End of Week Review   ☐ End of Month Review

Symbol	Setup Score	☐ L	Entry	Position Size	☐ TGT ☐ S/L	Execution Score
Setup		☐ S	Exit			

Symbol	Setup Score	☐ L	Entry	Position Size	☐ TGT ☐ S/L	Execution Score
Setup		☐ S	Exit			

Symbol	Setup Score	☐ L	Entry	Position Size	☐ TGT ☐ S/L	Execution Score
Setup		☐ S	Exit			

Symbol	Setup Score	☐ L	Entry	Position Size	☐ TGT ☐ S/L	Execution Score
Setup		☐ S	Exit			

Symbol	Setup Score	☐ L	Entry	Position Size	☐ TGT ☐ S/L	Execution Score
Setup		☐ S	Exit			

Symbol	Setup Score	☐ L	Entry	Position Size	☐ TGT ☐ S/L	Execution Score
Setup		☐ S	Exit			

Symbol	Setup Score	☐ L	Entry	Position Size	☐ TGT ☐ S/L	Execution Score
Setup		☐ S	Exit			

Symbol	Setup Score	☐ L	Entry	Position Size	☐ TGT ☐ S/L	Execution Score
Setup		☐ S	Exit			

Symbol	Setup Score	☐ L	Entry	Position Size	☐ TGT ☐ S/L	Execution Score
Setup		☐ S	Exit			

Symbol	Setup Score	☐ L	Entry	Position Size	☐ TGT ☐ S/L	Execution Score
Setup		☐ S	Exit			

Date   ☐ Paper ☐ Live

Watchlist

Market Events

Goals & Rewards

Pre-Market Observations

Post-Market Observations

☐ 24 Hour Review   ☐ End of Week Review   ☐ End of Month Review

Symbol	Setup Score	☐ L	Entry	Position Size	☐ TGT ☐ S/L	Execution Score
Setup		☐ S	Exit			

Symbol	Setup Score	☐ L	Entry	Position Size	☐ TGT ☐ S/L	Execution Score
Setup		☐ S	Exit			

Symbol	Setup Score	☐ L	Entry	Position Size	☐ TGT ☐ S/L	Execution Score
Setup		☐ S	Exit			

Symbol	Setup Score	☐ L	Entry	Position Size	☐ TGT ☐ S/L	Execution Score
Setup		☐ S	Exit			

Symbol	Setup Score	☐ L	Entry	Position Size	☐ TGT ☐ S/L	Execution Score
Setup		☐ S	Exit			

Symbol	Setup Score	☐ L	Entry	Position Size	☐ TGT ☐ S/L	Execution Score
Setup		☐ S	Exit			

Symbol	Setup Score	☐ L	Entry	Position Size	☐ TGT ☐ S/L	Execution Score
Setup		☐ S	Exit			

Symbol	Setup Score	☐ L	Entry	Position Size	☐ TGT ☐ S/L	Execution Score
Setup		☐ S	Exit			

Symbol	Setup Score	☐ L	Entry	Position Size	☐ TGT ☐ S/L	Execution Score
Setup		☐ S	Exit			

Symbol	Setup Score	☐ L	Entry	Position Size	☐ TGT ☐ S/L	Execution Score
Setup		☐ S	Exit			

| Date | ☐ Paper ☐ Live | Watchlist |

Market Events

Goals & Rewards

Pre-Market Observations

○ ○ ○ ○ ○ ○ ○ ○ ○ ○

Post-Market Observations

☐ 24 Hour Review   ☐ End of Week Review   ☐ End of Month Review

Symbol	Setup Score	☐ L	Entry	Position Size	☐ TGT ☐ S/L	Execution Score
Setup		☐ S	Exit			

Symbol	Setup Score	☐ L	Entry	Position Size	☐ TGT ☐ S/L	Execution Score
Setup		☐ S	Exit			

Symbol	Setup Score	☐ L	Entry	Position Size	☐ TGT ☐ S/L	Execution Score
Setup		☐ S	Exit			

Symbol	Setup Score	☐ L	Entry	Position Size	☐ TGT ☐ S/L	Execution Score
Setup		☐ S	Exit			

Symbol	Setup Score	☐ L	Entry	Position Size	☐ TGT ☐ S/L	Execution Score
Setup		☐ S	Exit			

Symbol	Setup Score	☐ L	Entry	Position Size	☐ TGT ☐ S/L	Execution Score
Setup		☐ S	Exit			

Symbol	Setup Score	☐ L	Entry	Position Size	☐ TGT ☐ S/L	Execution Score
Setup		☐ S	Exit			

Symbol	Setup Score	☐ L	Entry	Position Size	☐ TGT ☐ S/L	Execution Score
Setup		☐ S	Exit			

Symbol	Setup Score	☐ L	Entry	Position Size	☐ TGT ☐ S/L	Execution Score
Setup		☐ S	Exit			

Symbol	Setup Score	☐ L	Entry	Position Size	☐ TGT ☐ S/L	Execution Score
Setup		☐ S	Exit			

| Date | ☐ Paper ☐ Live | Watchlist |

Market Events

Goals & Rewards

Pre-Market Observations

○ ○ ○ ○ ○ ○ ○ ○ ○ ○

Post-Market Observations

☐ 24 Hour Review   ☐ End of Week Review   ☐ End of Month Review

Symbol	Setup Score	☐ L	Entry	Position Size	☐ TGT ☐ S/L	Execution Score
Setup		☐ S	Exit			

Symbol	Setup Score	☐ L	Entry	Position Size	☐ TGT ☐ S/L	Execution Score
Setup		☐ S	Exit			

Symbol	Setup Score	☐ L	Entry	Position Size	☐ TGT ☐ S/L	Execution Score
Setup		☐ S	Exit			

Symbol	Setup Score	☐ L	Entry	Position Size	☐ TGT ☐ S/L	Execution Score
Setup		☐ S	Exit			

Symbol	Setup Score	☐ L	Entry	Position Size	☐ TGT ☐ S/L	Execution Score
Setup		☐ S	Exit			

Symbol	Setup Score	☐ L	Entry	Position Size	☐ TGT ☐ S/L	Execution Score
Setup		☐ S	Exit			

Symbol	Setup Score	☐ L	Entry	Position Size	☐ TGT ☐ S/L	Execution Score
Setup		☐ S	Exit			

Symbol	Setup Score	☐ L	Entry	Position Size	☐ TGT ☐ S/L	Execution Score
Setup		☐ S	Exit			

Symbol	Setup Score	☐ L	Entry	Position Size	☐ TGT ☐ S/L	Execution Score
Setup		☐ S	Exit			

Symbol	Setup Score	☐ L	Entry	Position Size	☐ TGT ☐ S/L	Execution Score
Setup		☐ S	Exit			

| Date | ☐ Paper ☐ Live | Watchlist |

Market Events

Goals & Rewards

Pre-Market Observations

○ ○ ○ ○ ○ ○ ○ ○ ○ ○ ○

Post-Market Observations

☐ 24 Hour Review   ☐ End of Week Review   ☐ End of Month Review

Symbol	Setup Score	☐ L	Entry	Position Size	☐ TGT ☐ S/L	Execution Score
Setup		☐ S	Exit			

Symbol	Setup Score	☐ L	Entry	Position Size	☐ TGT ☐ S/L	Execution Score
Setup		☐ S	Exit			

Symbol	Setup Score	☐ L	Entry	Position Size	☐ TGT ☐ S/L	Execution Score
Setup		☐ S	Exit			

Symbol	Setup Score	☐ L	Entry	Position Size	☐ TGT ☐ S/L	Execution Score
Setup		☐ S	Exit			

Symbol	Setup Score	☐ L	Entry	Position Size	☐ TGT ☐ S/L	Execution Score
Setup		☐ S	Exit			

Symbol	Setup Score	☐ L	Entry	Position Size	☐ TGT ☐ S/L	Execution Score
Setup		☐ S	Exit			

Symbol	Setup Score	☐ L	Entry	Position Size	☐ TGT ☐ S/L	Execution Score
Setup		☐ S	Exit			

Symbol	Setup Score	☐ L	Entry	Position Size	☐ TGT ☐ S/L	Execution Score
Setup		☐ S	Exit			

Symbol	Setup Score	☐ L	Entry	Position Size	☐ TGT ☐ S/L	Execution Score
Setup		☐ S	Exit			

Symbol	Setup Score	☐ L	Entry	Position Size	☐ TGT ☐ S/L	Execution Score
Setup		☐ S	Exit			

Date

☐ Paper ☐ Live

Watchlist

Market Events

Goals & Rewards

Pre-Market Observations

Post-Market Observations

☐ 24 Hour Review ☐ End of Week Review ☐ End of Month Review

Symbol	Setup Score	☐ L	Entry	Position Size	☐ TGT ☐ S/L	Execution Score
Setup		☐ S	Exit			

Symbol	Setup Score	☐ L	Entry	Position Size	☐ TGT ☐ S/L	Execution Score
Setup		☐ S	Exit			

Symbol	Setup Score	☐ L	Entry	Position Size	☐ TGT ☐ S/L	Execution Score
Setup		☐ S	Exit			

Symbol	Setup Score	☐ L	Entry	Position Size	☐ TGT ☐ S/L	Execution Score
Setup		☐ S	Exit			

Symbol	Setup Score	☐ L	Entry	Position Size	☐ TGT ☐ S/L	Execution Score
Setup		☐ S	Exit			

Symbol	Setup Score	☐ L	Entry	Position Size	☐ TGT ☐ S/L	Execution Score
Setup		☐ S	Exit			

Symbol	Setup Score	☐ L	Entry	Position Size	☐ TGT ☐ S/L	Execution Score
Setup		☐ S	Exit			

Symbol	Setup Score	☐ L	Entry	Position Size	☐ TGT ☐ S/L	Execution Score
Setup		☐ S	Exit			

Symbol	Setup Score	☐ L	Entry	Position Size	☐ TGT ☐ S/L	Execution Score
Setup		☐ S	Exit			

Symbol	Setup Score	☐ L	Entry	Position Size	☐ TGT ☐ S/L	Execution Score
Setup		☐ S	Exit			

Date	☐ Paper ☐ Live

Market Events

Watchlist

Goals & Rewards

Pre-Market Observations

○ ○ ○ ○ ○ ○ ○ ○ ○ ○ ○

Post-Market Observations

☐ 24 Hour Review   ☐ End of Week Review   ☐ End of Month Review

Symbol		Setup Score	☐ L	Entry		Position Size	☐ TGT ☐ S/L	Execution Score
Setup			☐ S	Exit				

Symbol		Setup Score	☐ L	Entry		Position Size	☐ TGT ☐ S/L	Execution Score
Setup			☐ S	Exit				

Symbol		Setup Score	☐ L	Entry		Position Size	☐ TGT ☐ S/L	Execution Score
Setup			☐ S	Exit				

Symbol		Setup Score	☐ L	Entry		Position Size	☐ TGT ☐ S/L	Execution Score
Setup			☐ S	Exit				

Symbol		Setup Score	☐ L	Entry		Position Size	☐ TGT ☐ S/L	Execution Score
Setup			☐ S	Exit				

Symbol		Setup Score	☐ L	Entry		Position Size	☐ TGT ☐ S/L	Execution Score
Setup			☐ S	Exit				

Symbol		Setup Score	☐ L	Entry		Position Size	☐ TGT ☐ S/L	Execution Score
Setup			☐ S	Exit				

Symbol		Setup Score	☐ L	Entry		Position Size	☐ TGT ☐ S/L	Execution Score
Setup			☐ S	Exit				

Symbol		Setup Score	☐ L	Entry		Position Size	☐ TGT ☐ S/L	Execution Score
Setup			☐ S	Exit				

Symbol		Setup Score	☐ L	Entry		Position Size	☐ TGT ☐ S/L	Execution Score
Setup			☐ S	Exit				

| Date | ☐ Paper ☐ Live | Watchlist |

Market Events

Goals & Rewards

Pre-Market Observations

○ ○ ○ ○ ○ ○ ○ ○ ○ ○ ○

Post-Market Observations

☐ 24 Hour Review   ☐ End of Week Review   ☐ End of Month Review

Symbol	Setup Score	☐ L	Entry	Position Size	☐ TGT ☐ S/L	Execution Score
Setup		☐ S	Exit			

Symbol	Setup Score	☐ L	Entry	Position Size	☐ TGT ☐ S/L	Execution Score
Setup		☐ S	Exit			

Symbol	Setup Score	☐ L	Entry	Position Size	☐ TGT ☐ S/L	Execution Score
Setup		☐ S	Exit			

Symbol	Setup Score	☐ L	Entry	Position Size	☐ TGT ☐ S/L	Execution Score
Setup		☐ S	Exit			

Symbol	Setup Score	☐ L	Entry	Position Size	☐ TGT ☐ S/L	Execution Score
Setup		☐ S	Exit			

Symbol	Setup Score	☐ L	Entry	Position Size	☐ TGT ☐ S/L	Execution Score
Setup		☐ S	Exit			

Symbol	Setup Score	☐ L	Entry	Position Size	☐ TGT ☐ S/L	Execution Score
Setup		☐ S	Exit			

Symbol	Setup Score	☐ L	Entry	Position Size	☐ TGT ☐ S/L	Execution Score
Setup		☐ S	Exit			

Symbol	Setup Score	☐ L	Entry	Position Size	☐ TGT ☐ S/L	Execution Score
Setup		☐ S	Exit			

Symbol	Setup Score	☐ L	Entry	Position Size	☐ TGT ☐ S/L	Execution Score
Setup		☐ S	Exit			

| Date | ☐ Paper ☐ Live | Watchlist |

Market Events

Goals & Rewards

Pre-Market Observations

○ ○ ○ ○ ○ ○ ○ ○ ○ ○

Post-Market Observations

☐ 24 Hour Review   ☐ End of Week Review   ☐ End of Month Review

Symbol	Setup Score	☐ L	Entry	Position Size	☐ TGT ☐ S/L	Execution Score
Setup		☐ S	Exit			

Symbol	Setup Score	☐ L	Entry	Position Size	☐ TGT ☐ S/L	Execution Score
Setup		☐ S	Exit			

Symbol	Setup Score	☐ L	Entry	Position Size	☐ TGT ☐ S/L	Execution Score
Setup		☐ S	Exit			

Symbol	Setup Score	☐ L	Entry	Position Size	☐ TGT ☐ S/L	Execution Score
Setup		☐ S	Exit			

Symbol	Setup Score	☐ L	Entry	Position Size	☐ TGT ☐ S/L	Execution Score
Setup		☐ S	Exit			

Symbol	Setup Score	☐ L	Entry	Position Size	☐ TGT ☐ S/L	Execution Score
Setup		☐ S	Exit			

Symbol	Setup Score	☐ L	Entry	Position Size	☐ TGT ☐ S/L	Execution Score
Setup		☐ S	Exit			

Symbol	Setup Score	☐ L	Entry	Position Size	☐ TGT ☐ S/L	Execution Score
Setup		☐ S	Exit			

Symbol	Setup Score	☐ L	Entry	Position Size	☐ TGT ☐ S/L	Execution Score
Setup		☐ S	Exit			

Symbol	Setup Score	☐ L	Entry	Position Size	☐ TGT ☐ S/L	Execution Score
Setup		☐ S	Exit			

| Date | ☐ Paper ☐ Live | Watchlist |

Market Events

Goals & Rewards

Pre-Market Observations

○ ○ ○ ○ ○ ○ ○ ○ ○ ○

Post-Market Observations

☐ 24 Hour Review ☐ End of Week Review ☐ End of Month Review

Symbol	Setup Score	☐ L	Entry	Position Size	☐ TGT ☐ S/L	Execution Score
Setup		☐ S	Exit			

Symbol	Setup Score	☐ L	Entry	Position Size	☐ TGT ☐ S/L	Execution Score
Setup		☐ S	Exit			

Symbol	Setup Score	☐ L	Entry	Position Size	☐ TGT ☐ S/L	Execution Score
Setup		☐ S	Exit			

Symbol	Setup Score	☐ L	Entry	Position Size	☐ TGT ☐ S/L	Execution Score
Setup		☐ S	Exit			

Symbol	Setup Score	☐ L	Entry	Position Size	☐ TGT ☐ S/L	Execution Score
Setup		☐ S	Exit			

Symbol	Setup Score	☐ L	Entry	Position Size	☐ TGT ☐ S/L	Execution Score
Setup		☐ S	Exit			

Symbol	Setup Score	☐ L	Entry	Position Size	☐ TGT ☐ S/L	Execution Score
Setup		☐ S	Exit			

Symbol	Setup Score	☐ L	Entry	Position Size	☐ TGT ☐ S/L	Execution Score
Setup		☐ S	Exit			

Symbol	Setup Score	☐ L	Entry	Position Size	☐ TGT ☐ S/L	Execution Score
Setup		☐ S	Exit			

Symbol	Setup Score	☐ L	Entry	Position Size	☐ TGT ☐ S/L	Execution Score
Setup		☐ S	Exit			

| Date | ☐ Paper ☐ Live | Watchlist |

Market Events

Goals & Rewards

Pre-Market Observations

◯ ◯ ◯ ◯ ◯ ◯ ◯ ◯ ◯ ◯

Post-Market Observations

☐ 24 Hour Review   ☐ End of Week Review   ☐ End of Month Review

Symbol	Setup Score	☐ L	Entry	Position Size	☐ TGT ☐ S/L	Execution Score
Setup		☐ S	Exit			

Symbol	Setup Score	☐ L	Entry	Position Size	☐ TGT ☐ S/L	Execution Score
Setup		☐ S	Exit			

Symbol	Setup Score	☐ L	Entry	Position Size	☐ TGT ☐ S/L	Execution Score
Setup		☐ S	Exit			

Symbol	Setup Score	☐ L	Entry	Position Size	☐ TGT ☐ S/L	Execution Score
Setup		☐ S	Exit			

Symbol	Setup Score	☐ L	Entry	Position Size	☐ TGT ☐ S/L	Execution Score
Setup		☐ S	Exit			

Symbol	Setup Score	☐ L	Entry	Position Size	☐ TGT ☐ S/L	Execution Score
Setup		☐ S	Exit			

Symbol	Setup Score	☐ L	Entry	Position Size	☐ TGT ☐ S/L	Execution Score
Setup		☐ S	Exit			

Symbol	Setup Score	☐ L	Entry	Position Size	☐ TGT ☐ S/L	Execution Score
Setup		☐ S	Exit			

Symbol	Setup Score	☐ L	Entry	Position Size	☐ TGT ☐ S/L	Execution Score
Setup		☐ S	Exit			

Symbol	Setup Score	☐ L	Entry	Position Size	☐ TGT ☐ S/L	Execution Score
Setup		☐ S	Exit			

| Date | ☐ Paper ☐ Live | Watchlist |

Market Events

Goals & Rewards

Pre-Market Observations

○ ○ ○ ○ ○ ○ ○ ○ ○ ○ ○

Post-Market Observations

☐ 24 Hour Review   ☐ End of Week Review   ☐ End of Month Review

Symbol		Setup Score	☐ L	Entry		Position Size	☐ TGT ☐ S/L	Execution Score
Setup			☐ S	Exit				

Symbol		Setup Score	☐ L	Entry		Position Size	☐ TGT ☐ S/L	Execution Score
Setup			☐ S	Exit				

Symbol		Setup Score	☐ L	Entry		Position Size	☐ TGT ☐ S/L	Execution Score
Setup			☐ S	Exit				

Symbol		Setup Score	☐ L	Entry		Position Size	☐ TGT ☐ S/L	Execution Score
Setup			☐ S	Exit				

Symbol		Setup Score	☐ L	Entry		Position Size	☐ TGT ☐ S/L	Execution Score
Setup			☐ S	Exit				

Symbol		Setup Score	☐ L	Entry		Position Size	☐ TGT ☐ S/L	Execution Score
Setup			☐ S	Exit				

Symbol		Setup Score	☐ L	Entry		Position Size	☐ TGT ☐ S/L	Execution Score
Setup			☐ S	Exit				

Symbol		Setup Score	☐ L	Entry		Position Size	☐ TGT ☐ S/L	Execution Score
Setup			☐ S	Exit				

Symbol		Setup Score	☐ L	Entry		Position Size	☐ TGT ☐ S/L	Execution Score
Setup			☐ S	Exit				

Symbol		Setup Score	☐ L	Entry		Position Size	☐ TGT ☐ S/L	Execution Score
Setup			☐ S	Exit				

| Date | ☐ Paper ☐ Live | Watchlist |

Market Events

Goals & Rewards

Pre-Market Observations

○ ○ ○ ○ ○ ○ ○ ○ ○ ○ ○

Post-Market Observations

☐ 24 Hour Review   ☐ End of Week Review   ☐ End of Month Review

Symbol		Setup Score	☐ L	Entry		Position Size		☐ TGT ☐ S/L	Execution Score
Setup			☐ S	Exit					

Symbol		Setup Score	☐ L	Entry		Position Size		☐ TGT ☐ S/L	Execution Score
Setup			☐ S	Exit					

Symbol		Setup Score	☐ L	Entry		Position Size		☐ TGT ☐ S/L	Execution Score
Setup			☐ S	Exit					

Symbol		Setup Score	☐ L	Entry		Position Size		☐ TGT ☐ S/L	Execution Score
Setup			☐ S	Exit					

Symbol		Setup Score	☐ L	Entry		Position Size		☐ TGT ☐ S/L	Execution Score
Setup			☐ S	Exit					

Symbol		Setup Score	☐ L	Entry		Position Size		☐ TGT ☐ S/L	Execution Score
Setup			☐ S	Exit					

Symbol		Setup Score	☐ L	Entry		Position Size		☐ TGT ☐ S/L	Execution Score
Setup			☐ S	Exit					

Symbol		Setup Score	☐ L	Entry		Position Size		☐ TGT ☐ S/L	Execution Score
Setup			☐ S	Exit					

Symbol		Setup Score	☐ L	Entry		Position Size		☐ TGT ☐ S/L	Execution Score
Setup			☐ S	Exit					

Symbol		Setup Score	☐ L	Entry		Position Size		☐ TGT ☐ S/L	Execution Score
Setup			☐ S	Exit					

| Date | ☐ Paper ☐ Live | Watchlist |

Market Events

Goals & Rewards

Pre-Market Observations

◯ ◯ ◯ ◯ ◯ ◯ ◯ ◯ ◯ ◯ ◯

Post-Market Observations

☐ 24 Hour Review   ☐ End of Week Review   ☐ End of Month Review

Symbol	Setup Score	☐ L	Entry	Position Size	☐ TGT ☐ S/L	Execution Score
Setup		☐ S	Exit			

Symbol	Setup Score	☐ L	Entry	Position Size	☐ TGT ☐ S/L	Execution Score
Setup		☐ S	Exit			

Symbol	Setup Score	☐ L	Entry	Position Size	☐ TGT ☐ S/L	Execution Score
Setup		☐ S	Exit			

Symbol	Setup Score	☐ L	Entry	Position Size	☐ TGT ☐ S/L	Execution Score
Setup		☐ S	Exit			

Symbol	Setup Score	☐ L	Entry	Position Size	☐ TGT ☐ S/L	Execution Score
Setup		☐ S	Exit			

Symbol	Setup Score	☐ L	Entry	Position Size	☐ TGT ☐ S/L	Execution Score
Setup		☐ S	Exit			

Symbol	Setup Score	☐ L	Entry	Position Size	☐ TGT ☐ S/L	Execution Score
Setup		☐ S	Exit			

Symbol	Setup Score	☐ L	Entry	Position Size	☐ TGT ☐ S/L	Execution Score
Setup		☐ S	Exit			

Symbol	Setup Score	☐ L	Entry	Position Size	☐ TGT ☐ S/L	Execution Score
Setup		☐ S	Exit			

Symbol	Setup Score	☐ L	Entry	Position Size	☐ TGT ☐ S/L	Execution Score
Setup		☐ S	Exit			

Date	☐ Paper ☐ Live

Market Events

Watchlist

Goals & Rewards

Pre-Market Observations

○ ○ ○ ○ ○ ○ ○ ○ ○ ○

Post-Market Observations

☐ 24 Hour Review   ☐ End of Week Review   ☐ End of Month Review

Symbol	Setup Score	☐ L	Entry	Position Size	☐ TGT ☐ S/L	Execution Score
Setup		☐ S	Exit			

Symbol	Setup Score	☐ L	Entry	Position Size	☐ TGT ☐ S/L	Execution Score
Setup		☐ S	Exit			

Symbol	Setup Score	☐ L	Entry	Position Size	☐ TGT ☐ S/L	Execution Score
Setup		☐ S	Exit			

Symbol	Setup Score	☐ L	Entry	Position Size	☐ TGT ☐ S/L	Execution Score
Setup		☐ S	Exit			

Symbol	Setup Score	☐ L	Entry	Position Size	☐ TGT ☐ S/L	Execution Score
Setup		☐ S	Exit			

Symbol	Setup Score	☐ L	Entry	Position Size	☐ TGT ☐ S/L	Execution Score
Setup		☐ S	Exit			

Symbol	Setup Score	☐ L	Entry	Position Size	☐ TGT ☐ S/L	Execution Score
Setup		☐ S	Exit			

Symbol	Setup Score	☐ L	Entry	Position Size	☐ TGT ☐ S/L	Execution Score
Setup		☐ S	Exit			

Symbol	Setup Score	☐ L	Entry	Position Size	☐ TGT ☐ S/L	Execution Score
Setup		☐ S	Exit			

Symbol	Setup Score	☐ L	Entry	Position Size	☐ TGT ☐ S/L	Execution Score
Setup		☐ S	Exit			

| Date | ☐ Paper ☐ Live | Watchlist |

Market Events

Goals & Rewards

Pre-Market Observations

○ ○ ○ ○ ○ ○ ○ ○ ○ ○

Post-Market Observations

☐ 24 Hour Review ☐ End of Week Review ☐ End of Month Review

Symbol	Setup Score	☐ L	Entry	Position Size	☐ TGT ☐ S/L	Execution Score
Setup		☐ S	Exit			

Symbol	Setup Score	☐ L	Entry	Position Size	☐ TGT ☐ S/L	Execution Score
Setup		☐ S	Exit			

Symbol	Setup Score	☐ L	Entry	Position Size	☐ TGT ☐ S/L	Execution Score
Setup		☐ S	Exit			

Symbol	Setup Score	☐ L	Entry	Position Size	☐ TGT ☐ S/L	Execution Score
Setup		☐ S	Exit			

Symbol	Setup Score	☐ L	Entry	Position Size	☐ TGT ☐ S/L	Execution Score
Setup		☐ S	Exit			

Symbol	Setup Score	☐ L	Entry	Position Size	☐ TGT ☐ S/L	Execution Score
Setup		☐ S	Exit			

Symbol	Setup Score	☐ L	Entry	Position Size	☐ TGT ☐ S/L	Execution Score
Setup		☐ S	Exit			

Symbol	Setup Score	☐ L	Entry	Position Size	☐ TGT ☐ S/L	Execution Score
Setup		☐ S	Exit			

Symbol	Setup Score	☐ L	Entry	Position Size	☐ TGT ☐ S/L	Execution Score
Setup		☐ S	Exit			

Symbol	Setup Score	☐ L	Entry	Position Size	☐ TGT ☐ S/L	Execution Score
Setup		☐ S	Exit			

| Date | ☐ Paper ☐ Live | Watchlist |

Market Events

Goals & Rewards

Pre-Market Observations

○ ○ ○ ○ ○ ○ ○ ○ ○ ○ ○

Post-Market Observations

☐ 24 Hour Review ☐ End of Week Review ☐ End of Month Review

Symbol		Setup Score	☐ L	Entry		Position Size	☐ TGT ☐ S/L	Execution Score
Setup			☐ S	Exit				

Symbol		Setup Score	☐ L	Entry		Position Size	☐ TGT ☐ S/L	Execution Score
Setup			☐ S	Exit				

Symbol		Setup Score	☐ L	Entry		Position Size	☐ TGT ☐ S/L	Execution Score
Setup			☐ S	Exit				

Symbol		Setup Score	☐ L	Entry		Position Size	☐ TGT ☐ S/L	Execution Score
Setup			☐ S	Exit				

Symbol		Setup Score	☐ L	Entry		Position Size	☐ TGT ☐ S/L	Execution Score
Setup			☐ S	Exit				

Symbol		Setup Score	☐ L	Entry		Position Size	☐ TGT ☐ S/L	Execution Score
Setup			☐ S	Exit				

Symbol		Setup Score	☐ L	Entry		Position Size	☐ TGT ☐ S/L	Execution Score
Setup			☐ S	Exit				

Symbol		Setup Score	☐ L	Entry		Position Size	☐ TGT ☐ S/L	Execution Score
Setup			☐ S	Exit				

Symbol		Setup Score	☐ L	Entry		Position Size	☐ TGT ☐ S/L	Execution Score
Setup			☐ S	Exit				

Symbol		Setup Score	☐ L	Entry		Position Size	☐ TGT ☐ S/L	Execution Score
Setup			☐ S	Exit				

| Date | ☐ Paper ☐ Live | Watchlist |

Market Events

Goals & Rewards

Pre-Market Observations

○ ○ ○ ○ ○ ○ ○ ○ ○ ○

Post-Market Observations

☐ 24 Hour Review   ☐ End of Week Review   ☐ End of Month Review

Symbol	Setup Score	☐ L	Entry	Position Size	☐ TGT ☐ S/L	Execution Score
Setup		☐ S	Exit			

Symbol	Setup Score	☐ L	Entry	Position Size	☐ TGT ☐ S/L	Execution Score
Setup		☐ S	Exit			

Symbol	Setup Score	☐ L	Entry	Position Size	☐ TGT ☐ S/L	Execution Score
Setup		☐ S	Exit			

Symbol	Setup Score	☐ L	Entry	Position Size	☐ TGT ☐ S/L	Execution Score
Setup		☐ S	Exit			

Symbol	Setup Score	☐ L	Entry	Position Size	☐ TGT ☐ S/L	Execution Score
Setup		☐ S	Exit			

Symbol	Setup Score	☐ L	Entry	Position Size	☐ TGT ☐ S/L	Execution Score
Setup		☐ S	Exit			

Symbol	Setup Score	☐ L	Entry	Position Size	☐ TGT ☐ S/L	Execution Score
Setup		☐ S	Exit			

Symbol	Setup Score	☐ L	Entry	Position Size	☐ TGT ☐ S/L	Execution Score
Setup		☐ S	Exit			

Symbol	Setup Score	☐ L	Entry	Position Size	☐ TGT ☐ S/L	Execution Score
Setup		☐ S	Exit			

Symbol	Setup Score	☐ L	Entry	Position Size	☐ TGT ☐ S/L	Execution Score
Setup		☐ S	Exit			

| Date | ☐ Paper ☐ Live | Watchlist |

Market Events

Goals & Rewards

Pre-Market Observations

○ ○ ○ ○ ○ ○ ○ ○ ○ ○

Post-Market Observations

☐ 24 Hour Review ☐ End of Week Review ☐ End of Month Review

Symbol	Setup Score	☐ L	Entry	Position Size	☐ TGT ☐ S/L	Execution Score
Setup		☐ S	Exit			

Symbol	Setup Score	☐ L	Entry	Position Size	☐ TGT ☐ S/L	Execution Score
Setup		☐ S	Exit			

Symbol	Setup Score	☐ L	Entry	Position Size	☐ TGT ☐ S/L	Execution Score
Setup		☐ S	Exit			

Symbol	Setup Score	☐ L	Entry	Position Size	☐ TGT ☐ S/L	Execution Score
Setup		☐ S	Exit			

Symbol	Setup Score	☐ L	Entry	Position Size	☐ TGT ☐ S/L	Execution Score
Setup		☐ S	Exit			

Symbol	Setup Score	☐ L	Entry	Position Size	☐ TGT ☐ S/L	Execution Score
Setup		☐ S	Exit			

Symbol	Setup Score	☐ L	Entry	Position Size	☐ TGT ☐ S/L	Execution Score
Setup		☐ S	Exit			

Symbol	Setup Score	☐ L	Entry	Position Size	☐ TGT ☐ S/L	Execution Score
Setup		☐ S	Exit			

Symbol	Setup Score	☐ L	Entry	Position Size	☐ TGT ☐ S/L	Execution Score
Setup		☐ S	Exit			

Symbol	Setup Score	☐ L	Entry	Position Size	☐ TGT ☐ S/L	Execution Score
Setup		☐ S	Exit			

Goals & Rewards

Goals & Rewards

Printed in France by Amazon
Brétigny-sur-Orge, FR

14231811R00080